The Wou

Dr Peter Schellenbaum was born in 1939. After studying theology, he worked as a student pastor in Munich between 1971 and 1975. He then went on to train in psychoanalysis at the C. G. Jung Institute in Zurich where he now holds the position of lecturer and teaching analyst. He also runs his own private psychotherapy practice in Zurich.

The Wound
of the Unloved

Releasing the Life Energy

PETER SCHELLENBAUM

Translated by Tim Nevill

ELEMENT BOOKS

© 1988 Kosel-Verlag GmbH & Co, Munchen
Translation © Tim Nevill 1990

First published in 1988

This edition first published in 1990 by
Element Books Limited
Longmead, Shaftesbury, Dorset

Designed by Jenny Liddle
Typeset by Selectmove Ltd, London
Printed and bound by Billings,
Hylton Road, Worcester
Cover design by Max Fairbrother
Cover illustration by Janine McNamara

British Library Cataloguing in Publication Data
Schellenbaum, Peter 1939–
The wound of the unloved
1. Self-discovery
I. Title
158',1

ISBN 1-85230-124-4

Contents

A Prefatory Note — vii

PART ONE ● **Unloved** — 1

1. The Oldest Wound — 3
2. 'The Wrong Person Again!' and Other Unloved
   Games — 13
3. 'Everyone Loves Me' and Other Unloved Games — 21
4. Psycho-Energetics — 30
   Concept and Experience of Life-Energy — 30
   Magnetism and Psycho-Energetics — 38

PART TWO ● **Understanding** — 47

5. Love of Outcasts — 49
6. Renunciation of Belated Parental Love — 59
7. The Open Wound of Depression — 69
8. Identity in Longing — 80

PART THREE ● **Sensing** — 93

9. Pressure and Impulse — 95
10. The Word Becomes Flesh — 105
11. Traumatic and Erotic Patterns — 116
12. Participation in the Suffering of the Unloved Child — 131

PART FOUR • **Liberating**   141

13. Mental Massage or the Purring Cat   143
14. Love is Abnormal   155
15. Essential Solitude   163
16. The Energetics of Love   175

Notes   184

Bibliography   188

A Prefatory Note

In order to do justice to the theme of *The Wound of the Unloved* I have to involve the whole of myself: as a human being with his own life story; as a psychotherapist who out of choice and for professional reasons comes into close contact with a large number of people; as an analyst convinced that philosophy, literature, and mysticism must save psychology from a degree of narrowness; and as a practitioner who needs critical theory. If one or more of those areas were excluded, I wouldn't cover as much ground as the theme demands. So in this book I bring together stories from my life, case histories (changed for the sake of discretion) and interpretations of dreams from my work as psychotherapist, dialogues with clients which can be read as inner dialogues, philosophical reflections, illustrations from literature, mystical insights, and theoretical clarifications. Viewed from outside, that may perhaps seem a confusing mixture of various starting points, but from within it reflects the interconnections between the vital individual and the expansiveness of human existence. The psyche is richer than all of psychology's systematisations.

In this book I continue to pursue the development of a psychology of movement: psycho-energetics. Aspects of living a fully human existence – whose interrelationships do not appear in a state of rest – flow together in a shared movement.

I would like to express special thanks to:

- all those I was privileged to follow as a psychotherapist and analyst. They led me to crucial insights.
- Peter Sloterdijk, master of living speech, who helped me find expression for what I wanted to say.
- Stephano Sabetti for vital impulses.
- Heike, my wife, for all the challenges.
- Heidi Widmer for fresh stimulation in an old friendship. The title for this book arose during a conversation with her.
- Georg Wachtler for many ideas and much encouragement.
- Dörthe Binkert for prompting thought and imagination.
- Gerda Boyesen who made an insight possible at an important point.
- the friends of the Nietzsche Study Group at Sils-Maria in September 1987.

Peter Schellenbaum
Zürich, May 1988

Part One

Unloved

ONE

The Oldest Wound

A couple of days ago an acquaintance asked me whether the book I wanted to write would, like its predecessors, be concerned with both the problems of the people in therapy with me and my own difficulties, thereby aiming at making possible a process of maturation within myself as well as in the reader, healing my own wound of being unloved. I immediately answered: 'No, not this time.' As I said this I thought: 'Recently I have attained "peace" and have become more satisfied. I have clarified old relationships and gained new ones. Even when I'm alone, I still feel connected with many people and the world. No, this time I am mainly writing for other people. In addition I want to make more concrete and expand the beginnings of psycho-energetics therapy as presented in *Abschied von der Selbstzerstörung* (*Farewell to Self-Destruction*), situating it within the history of ideas.' 'No', I told my acquaintance again, 'I no longer suffer from the wound of being unloved. That was the most painful of all the wounds of my childhood, but I worked on it during my training analysis and then in ongoing self-analyses. The wound of being unloved no longer torments me.'

But then, last night, I had the following dream. I was standing with many other people (mainly of importance from my childhood days) in a gloomy, dreary room. Someone said to me: 'Look at yourself, how run down you are! You've become increasingly more frail since that serious operation three years ago. Your eyes are dull and look unhealthy. You're going downhill, and your strength is declining.' To my left is a woman who attracts me. But she too regards me dully and impassively. I suddenly know that no one loves me. I am irrevocably separated from everyone. This is hell. This mounting sense of deadness is my ultimate way of suffering.

I woke up and remembered that when I had arrived in Italy around midnight, Tellaro in no way accorded with my expectations. A hurricane-like storm was raging so that I had to stay sitting in my car for half an hour before I could unload the books and other things I'd brought along. I was hardly out of the car when a gust of wind tore the umbrella out of my hand. Everything got wet. Once I was in the house I opened my room's window to the sea, and the foam from a huge breaking wave sprayed my face, covering the desk with innumerable tiny drops. I really hadn't reckoned with being assailed like this, or with the onslaught in my dream.

I gradually calmed down, understanding that in the dream destructive pain over something long past had once again broken through like a raging torrent, and also comprehending that I had myself become similar to the woman in that dream, unrelated to my energy, my organism, and to the others. What had become overgrown or been healed was torn open once again, and had started to bleed. The wound of being unloved was not dead in me. It will not die as long as I live.

Now, at midday, the dark water is glittering before me, vibrating dizzyingly beneath the powerful sun. This splendour would not be so refreshing without last night's storm. The wound of being unloved no longer torments. But the vivid memory of its pain makes possible the light I want to throw on the subject of this book.

Some people never manage, throughout their whole lives, to think, let alone to say: 'My mother didn't love me', or 'My father didn't love me', or 'My mother and father didn't love me', or simply 'I am unloved' – even though they may feel that. That single sentence seems so terrible, so destructive, that it cannot even be expressed within the silence of inner dialogue. Its decisive truth nevertheless constantly forces its way into expression. Dulled knowledge of one's own state of being 'unloved' finds complicated roundabout ways into the open because the shortest way of direct expression is blocked. As psychologically 'enlightened' human beings we perhaps have no inhibitions about saying that as children we were left alone on this or that occasion, that we were not understood, that our parents were overburdened or ill, that narrow religious convictions made them fearful, that they made excessive demands of us, that they were unable to respond to our particular abilities, and so on. *The Drama of the Gifted Child* (Alice Miller) becomes subject matter for conversations. From time to time we change the arguments whereby we seek to explain and get rid of fundamental discontent with ourselves. Like poor souls in pursuit of redemption, we wander restlessly from explanation to explanation. But the charge of energy is more massive than what is expressed in words. On our tortuous path towards freedom we obfuscate the clear, simple truth: 'I was unloved and still am'. That is a truth which also applies to those who were loved too much or wrongly. Lack of love has many masks. This truth applies too – in a profound sense which I shall elucidate – to people who were 'sufficiently loved'. The wound of the unloved is the wound of human existence.

Or else we reduce the explosive power of such declarations by filtering them through psychological jargon. We then perhaps say that we are symbiotic, suffer from the frustrations of early childhood, lack empathy, or have a narcissistic wound. We thus make use of psychology so as to avoid the massive primordial pain of: 'My mother didn't love me', or 'My father didn't love me', or 'My mother and father didn't love me', or simply 'I'm unloved'.

We at most manage – maintaining a rational distance from our feelings and striving for objectivity – to say: 'I was wrongly, or insufficiently, or excessively loved'. From an objective viewpoint that way of expressing things is certainly more correct. How would we otherwise have survived infancy? But we are not objects, and the language of feelings, revealing and healing the facts of feelings, does not know any objective 'on the one hand . . . on the other'. A feeling that erupts openly is complete and undivided. The girl whose mother tells her not to take part in boys' games, despite that being the daughter's dearest wish, feels completely unloved as she sits there crying. The pain is undivided. She doesn't tell herself: 'My parents partly like me, partly not. They like me in the role of a girl, but not as a boy'. That sentence is not, however, even objectively correct. Joy in 'naughty children' who throw overboard social conventions is the characteristic distinguishing between conscious, genuine love, accepting the child as it is, and blind adoration. We may not require

5

love for biological survival but we do need it for psychological development. This mother didn't really love her child!

I say that someone is *'unloved'* if his or her inability to live fully derives from a basic feeling of being unloved. That is the case in all more profound psychological disturbances, particularly where narcissism is involved. That feeling is repressed because it is so decisive. If it is finally conceded, its dominance becomes apparent. The associated intensity varies in accordance with the underlying events in childhood and one's own predisposition and current life situation. The sense of being unloved does not exclude other feelings whose positive nature allows them to be conscious and approved of. And yet it is that sense of being unloved which must become conscious. To express such a feeling marks the beginning of healing. That is why the over-simplified characterisation of people who suffer from that, and this book's title of *The Wound of the Unloved*, are justified. The wound of the unloved is the cause of a lack of 'basic trust' (Erik Erikson). If we want to alleviate that, we must face up to that wound.

UNLOVED GAMES

This book is intended to bring the pain of being unloved back into the body, seeing through that pain right down to its existential depths, and admitting all its repercussions into awareness, so as finally to become free of it. The first task is to clarify the forms of obfuscation – I call them 'unloved games' – with which we keep that pain at a distance. In the first part – the first four chapters – I endeavour to make conscious the fact of being unloved, but at this stage without further explanations and therapeutic suggestions. In the second part – chapters five to eight – I strive to transmit understanding of how the feeling of being unloved comes into being. In the third part – chapters nine to twelve – I indicate a way in which what has come into existence can be made to vanish, and the feeling of being unloved can be dissolved by living through the complete range of emotions involved, which the persons concerned have previously avoided. In the fourth part – chapters thirteen to sixteen – the wound of the unloved is presented as something profoundly existential and the fundamental characteristic of the human predicament.

I therefore chose the following brief titles for the four parts of the book: *Unloved – Understanding – Sensing – Liberating.* This way accords with the four steps taken when solving a psychological problem. Initially we are entangled and imprisoned in that problem. Then we distance ourselves from it, attempting to understand its origins. Next we deliberately entrust ourselves to the flood of emotions, images, and gestures forcing their way into existence. Finally we liberate ourselves so as to lead the genuinely human existence which was previously denied us.

Verbal therapies and analyses often remain stuck in the phase of understanding. They probably provide a number of insights and breakthroughs into the flourishing land of emotionality, but then call for a return to what is orderly and analysable. Body-oriented therapies mostly skip that second phase of thorough investigation, or are incapable of meeting its demands, so that emotional experiencing gradually degenerates into a sterile going through the motions. Psychoenergetics aims at making possible interaction between reason and emotion in a single natural process without either being curtailed. I will explain that in the fourth chapter.

The previously mentioned four stages of therapy were inspired by the teachings of the Buddha[1]. For him the first step involves 'alertness' to real 'circumstances'; the second, observation of their 'stages of development'; the third leads to experience of 'states of transience'; and the fourth brings about capacity to prevent the initial situation coming into existence again. I am not concerned with comparing the contents of this book to Buddhist teachings, but rather with the psychological process expressed in these four stages: from the uncovering of our repressive activities to the greatest possible insight into what really happened during our childhood and is still happening today, then to what wants to live out of us as a matter of inner necessity, and finally to liberation from slavery to former patterns of existence. The order entailed in this simple model of human maturation allows what is disorderly – that is, everything pertaining to love and its absence – to unfold little by little.

Viewed in social terms, the wound of the unloved involves the *dubious denials* which a human being takes on in apathetically submitting to the rules of family, nation, culture, and religion, rejecting those aspects of human expression society has not accepted. Such enforced submission is then passed on to the next generation, which first suffers, then keeps silence, and finally, like its parents, make others suffer. In his examination of magnetism, Peter Sloterdijk characterises the civilised human being as a 'swamp of stagnant negativity'[2]. Magnetism is the original form of modern psychotherapy (chapter 4), viewing the human body as being equipped with inner knowledge of health and sickness rather than as merely Descartes' 'extended object'. If we have access to the body's knowledge, we are also aware of the necessary revolutions, opposing the dubious denials. The rules of society are then recognised as what they really are: conventions which, unlike fixed norms, can be changed when they do more harm than good. The closer we come to liberation from our feeling of being unloved, the more we will allow fossilised norms to burst like boils. It is 'normal' to be unloved because norms do not affirm important aspects of what is loveable within ourselves and others. Love, on the other hand, is 'abnormal' (title of chapter 14) because it also accepts what the norm denies.

A SOCIAL PHENOMENON

The wound of the unloved is therefore not just a private matter affecting those who lacked love and are now unable to love. It is a social phenomenon. Parents who cannot love the otherness of their children are led astray by social conventions and the resultant anxieties about life. Love, inclusive of parental love, is the most natural thing in the world. We do not have to struggle for that. It flows of its own accord if we do not close ourselves to life. Unblocked existence releases love. Life-energy is love – both of oneself and of others. People merely licked into shape by norms have to reject that idea as being idealistic. But don't they too experience more love during periods of greater casualness and vitality? No, we must mainly be concerned with the obstacles to love, with the circumstances in which love is wounded. Everything else looks after itself. It's true that I will also write about love but only in order to strengthen and provide verbal support for what streams forth spontaneously when we just allow it. Faithfulness to norms and lack of love go together, so the place where therapy occurs must not be a refuge from social realities. It must, on the contrary, be a space where the individual becomes more aware of himself or herself as a point of intersection between what is one's own and what comes from outside. Only then can scope for previously unloved aspects of our humanity open up.

There is one feeling which should alert parents if ascertained in their child: *shame*. Shame is the feeling which develops where there is conflict between the individual and society. We cover up and do not love whatever we are ashamed of. We are afraid of the *disgrace*, and of being ignominiously rejected. What is socially frowned upon awakens shame in the individual. Such socially conditioned shame is not to be confused with natural reticence, which we sometimes need in order to come to ourselves and remain there. People who are often ashamed in company are not free, do not love themselves, and incline to excessive identification with idealised others – and to depression. Their wound is that of being unloved. How sad that woman's organ of sexual contact is known as the 'pudenda' – something she has to be ashamed of. Women's depressions often arise in connection with this area of sexuality, which is covered up and shut off from contact. And doesn't what is shameful arouse aggression in inhibited men, sometimes to the point of wanting to rape? Confronted with that, the woman sees confirmation of her shame, covers herself up even more, and loves herself even less. The vicious circle of social prudery and narrow mindedness, of individual shame and violence, thus gets under way.

We are all ashamed of what is unloved within ourselves, whether it be a particular part of the body ('fat thighs'), or a specific characteristic such as a boy's ridiculed liking for playing with dolls, which cannot unfold its paradoxical significance, capacity for transformation, and potential so long as we are merely ashamed. That even applies to behaviour rightly punished by society. As always, the part stands for the whole, and contempt for a single aspect of ourselves entails scorning our entire being. We should turn towards and favour the wound of the unloved rather than running away from it. The focus of our suffering can then become the source of our vitality.

When she was engaged in the process of writing Virginia Woolf felt alive, but after reading the completed work she was regularly overcome by shame. She was a woman living at a time of social change. Unlike millions of other women in her generation, she opened her mouth, but then she was ashamed of her words. The wound of the unloved thus kept festering. Virginia Woolf killed herself in 1941 shortly after completing her novel *Between the Acts*[3].

It is difficult to stand by the words that have come from deep within ourselves just as it is difficult to maintain living eye contact. People who were unloved as children have difficulty in loving themselves under the gaze of another person. If they do not succeed in that, they continue to experience themselves as being unloved even though the contrary may be true. They become lively and creative when they do manage to remain within the magnetic field of an exchange of looks. I will show how we can learn from the critical 'view-point' where everything is decided to endure this tension, go further, and remain on the trail of energy and pleasure in life (chapters 9 and 10).

There are always extreme cases demonstrating the entire range of a problem, people where the wound of being unloved is so long-established and deep that it sets the entire psychological personality on fire, leading to psychosis. In her book *On Human Symbiosis and the Vicissitudes of Individuation*, Margaret Mahler tells of a seven year old boy who after the sudden loss of his mother – from whom he had not yet separated as is usual in his age group – clung to some beer barrels so as 'to re-establish and repair the broken off contact with his pregnant mother'[4] and finally became psychotic. As long as the 'symbiotic object', as Freud writes, is still experienced as an integral part of one's own ego, its loss includes the threat of self-destruction. The wound of the unloved always occurs at a time when we are symbiotically linked with another person – interconnected, and grown and knotted together. If such intertwining is great, the wound caused by a loss of love digs itself in deeply, and we only experience ourselves in pain and destruction. Sometimes it seems as if that could also happen in a failed love affair between two adults. But if it happens there, then it happened earlier in childhood and adolescence.

The peak and turning-point within the symbiotic phase is during the third quarter of the first year of life. The child then starts to distinguish itself from the mother, and to feel itself to be an individual. This phase lasts about two years, leading to 'the child's developmental readiness for independent and separate functioning accompanied by joy'[5]. A more or less intensive fusion with the parents does nevertheless persist throughout childhood and adolescence, and often even longer. An individual who has become independent is, however, no longer threatened with total destruction as the result of later love wounds.

AFFECTING ADULT RELATIONSHIPS

The way in which we were not loved during childhood can be directly read from our adult relationships. Anyone who knows how to decipher the behavioural patterns of the unloved thereby derives more accurate information about the nature and place of the wound than by assembling childhood memories. Any conversation should therefore always take the current situation as its starting point, and regularly return to that. In addition there is the fact that wounds from the preverbal phase cannot be conveyed by way of words. Therapy is here primarily concerned with bringing emotionality to life (chapter 12). I only want to relativise, not devalue, childhood memories. Bringing such memories to light remains an important objective in the process of human maturation, not least because their resurrection leads to our experiencing ourselves in a developmental context with all its history of life enhancement and inhibitions.

Wherever we were not loved, we do not love ourselves. Blind spots in our self knowledge correspond to lack of self-love. The Delphic oracle's basic principle of 'Know thyself!' must be complemented by 'Love thyself!' since knowledge and love are psychologically inseparable. One of the basic principles in psycho-energetics is that the therapist 'contacts' and boosts the client's self-love and self-knowledge (chapter 4) by relating to his or her emotional pressures.

We recognise someone unloved by the fact that he *mirrors* other people where he does not love and know himself. 'He strove to learn how one feels and has emotions by mirroring others and himself', writes Margaret Mahler about an emotionless young man. She calls this process *mirror identification*. According to Mahler, the unloved unceasingly seek their mother in everyone approached whose eyes are expected to reflect love for them. That gives rise to emotional dependence and an incapacity to see and feel a partner as another. I seek a way out of the mirror identification through *reflection of a model* (chapter 8). Passive dependence on the reflecting reference person is meant to become active self-experiencing in the mirror of a suitable model.

The wound of the unloved receives expression in the painful feeling of being *rejected* rather than loved (chapter 5). That feeling is, however, often unrealistic with regard to the actual situation. The unloved – in the psychological sense of the word as used here – are often loved and accepted just as much as other people. So long as it lasts, the feeling of being unloved – despite reality saying otherwise – indicates an emotional incapacity to love oneself.

TWO

'The Wrong Person Again!' and Other Unloved Games

I apply the term 'unloved' to people who at a critical point in their life – usually during childhood and adolescence – have had a traumatic experience with love, which penetrated their personality structure and now colours and influences all emotional relationships. In every later relationship the 'unloved' programme automatically enters into individual behaviour patterns. The first step in therapy consists of recognising the existence of such a programme and distinguishing its nature. It is wrong to want to explain and interpret everything right from the start. Only when a feeling for wrong programming has become part of the client's make-up can the therapist's interpretation establish detachment from the course of events bringing about unhappiness, and uncover access to new experiences of feeling.

Therapies where little time is devoted to this initial phase of careful stocktaking are like luxuriant water plants which wilt as quickly as they grow. Indulgence in profound insights and experiences is followed by disillusionment and disappointment. The uncovering of one's own 'script' – as transactional analysis calls the life plan that causes illness – is of course insufficient on its own. But this small first step is indispensable as the basis for progressing further. It is also amusing to pursue one's own games *ad absurdum* by way of consequential exaggeration within the kind of dialectical discussion Socrates loved. Laughter is the beginning of change. Most clients initially experience therapy as a demand for achievement. As long as that is the case, the unhappiness programme, which led them to therapy, will persist. Astonishing transformations often happen where people laugh a lot. I will therefore employ a degree of irony – rather than grand pathos – in describing the games played by the unloved as the 'unloved games'. This irony does not derive from disdain for the people I work with, but from a liking which doesn't allow itself to be duped and destroyed by the individuals' unkindness towards themselves.

In this and the following chapter I shall describe a number of widespread unloved games. The fact that someone has attained virtuoso skill in one of these by no means signifies that he does not also possess above-average skill in others. Perhaps he has developed his own original synthesis out of several games. All these games have in common a link between two contradictory strivings. One of them is the trauma, the formative psychological wound from childhood, which says: 'No, love does not exist' – and the other is the ego, which desperately counters with: 'But yes, love must exist'. Out of that contradiction there arises a 'cohabitation', which only seems natural to us when we are ourselves at home and trapped in this ambivalence. And we are constantly trapped so long as the 'No' of the internal partner within this conflict silences the other's 'Yes', and vice-versa. That is how the celebrated double-bind (Gregory Bateson) comes into existence.

Pierre de Ronsard writes in a love poem: 'Si c'est un malheur, baste, je délibère/ de vivre malheureux en si belle misère'. Freely translated this runs: 'Yes, it is a misfortune, but I decide to live unhappily in this beautiful misery'. It sometimes seems as if the unloved incline towards that attitude. The pleasure derived from unloved games is often considerable. The ego picks all the currants out of the unsuccessful cake, but conceals them from the therapist. Only a happy facial expression when telling of the recurrence of unhappy love games sometimes betrays the secret currants on which clients feast. 'Wouldn't life lose all interest if it became simpler?' such born actors seem to ask. The difficulty at the start of any therapy involves inability as yet to imagine the 'other'. In therapeutic discussions, the bad games must be pursued to the extreme so that the resultant displeasure is accompanied by a breakthrough to consciousness of these processes as unloved games. I describe the first game in greater detail than the others since they all have some things in common.

'THE WRONG PERSON AGAIN!'

The first unloved game is called 'The wrong person again!'. A twenty-five year old cultivated woman had already fallen in love many times with obviously older men. They were all flashy, uncouth, uncontrolled, ruthless businessmen yet tender and warm in love like teddy bears. That at least is how the woman portrayed them. The initial feeling of happiness, deriving from cosy closeness and animal warmth, only lasted for a short time. In the first act of the drama sexuality played little or no part. The woman sank into infinite security: she as it were dug herself into this male corpulence, and regained her health in this confidence-engendering mass. She was unreservedly happy, asserting that this man essentially offered what she had always sought. On him she could build her existence. And she began to concoct plans for establishing a life together with her new friend. If he lived in another town, she was immediately ready to move there and give up her previous circle of friends.

But things never got that far. In the second act of the drama, there suddenly developed a profound contempt for the man who had just been idolised. This sudden contempt constituted her entire sense of being alive. She now wanted to sleep with him. She harrassed and humiliated him through sexuality. If he demonstrated the slightest sign of tiredness, she made sarcastic fun of his age. Or she refused to sleep with him when she sensed he really wanted that. Of course, all this occurred without any deliberate intentions being involved.

In the third act she reaped the fruits of her contempt – not from the man, who had not begun to understand what was happening to him in these rapid changes, but from within herself. Passion declined and burnt out. She was then seized by anxiety about having to part company with this friend, so she struggled to be nice, made herself sleep with him, flattered him with a bad conscience, and gave him presents.

Dislike intensified, however, so that the transition to the fourth and final act occurred contrary to her wishes. She could only behave as she did. She had to drop this man too.

After she had done that, she withdrew, became apathetic and impassive, ate a great deal, slept a lot, attempted to forget and eradicate what she had experienced, until she could finally express with complete conviction the sentence that released her from all guilt, humiliation, and reflection: 'He was simply not the right man! The wrong person again!' – for the sixth time already. It was true that she had always, since her childhood, been seeking 'this man'. In other words she was looking for a 'father' who did not coldly keep an emotional distance as her real father had; a man without the polished, soulless manners she was familiar with; a man who stood his ground, bull-like and potently, ruthless with everyone but good to her, unlike her actual father who was indifferent to her and considerate towards others. Only this fleshy, carnal teddy bear could redeem her from the depleted ghost her father was. But, despite everything, she still loved her real father, yearning for him! The question is: how can she please him? During the second phase her father started to exert a renewed impact, increasingly drawing upon her energy – drawing her into a complex (C.G. Jung) which locks up energy and starves life. She despised what she needed. She unmanned the person whose strength she required. Yet the pleasure in closeness persisted and her feelings were still strong, albeit focusing on contempt. This second phase involved the brief total union of the two contradictory strivings in her heart: towards this man who rescued her from her father and towards the father who punished his rival. Both were united by delight in contempt. In the third and fourth phases, the father routed the rescuer, thereby reversing the initial situation. The circle thus completed itself: a game without end, lust for life fizzling out in denial of life.

The woman and I played through the four acts, extending each in the imagination to the limits of the bearable: the period of security up to the point of loss of will power and self-determination, the time of contempt up to destruction of what she most needed, the period of artificial striving for what had already been lost, inclusive of a grotesque, contorted politeness taken over from her father, and the time of apathy after the separation leading to a feeling of total meaninglessness—with the result that, in the pain of fresh awareness, she finally no longer uttered the often repeated cry of 'The wrong person again!'. The wound of being unloved was now out in the open, and she could relate to it.

'SO THAT YOU LOVE ME'

The second unloved game is called: *'So that you love me'*. Parents have no more effective way of training their children than by dosing the amount of love given or withheld. The apron strings of love are more effective than the trainer's whip. Someone who as a child had to court love is predestined as an adult for the 'So that you love me' game. Such love relationships have affinities with the fisherman in Goethe's ballad: 'She half dragged him down/he half sank/and he was never seen again'. Men and women who love too much play this second unloved game. They adapt to one another passively, submit, do everything to please, and live in constant fear that the other may leave them. Their dependence can go as far as in the case of the woman who succumbed to total panic that her husband might be clearing off when he had to go to the lavatory. Like the fisherman in Goethe's ballad, the true personality goes under in this game. Such people no longer sense their vitality, what Meister Eckhart calls the 'spark of the soul'. They become insecure to the point of desperation. There are many variations of this unloved game, and I will mention two.

The first is the *achievement variation*. During childhood its victims were valued in terms of social success. Parental love was dependent on good marks at school. Even later as adults their efforts are motivated by fear of withdrawal of love rather than delight in challenges. Spontaneity never gets a look in because it can only flourish within unpremeditatedly benevolent surroundings. People who play the 'So that you love me' game attempt to gain love through compulsive endeavours, adaptation, and work, thereby becoming dry and embittered, and are ultimately pushed aside. After all, how can one love such a tense, unspontaneous, and overwhelmingly fearful human being? The fears of a person hungry for love are thus confirmed. After a transitional phase of desperation, he or she then seeks a new partner whose love has once again to be earned if anxiety does not lead to retreat. The person concerned gives more and more but can take less and less since self-respect declines with every fresh onslaught of lovesickness.

The *disciplinary variation* is the second form of the 'So that you love me' unloved game. Gerda Boyesen writes that her parents time and again admonished her not to cry. She thus clenched her teeth 'so that you love me'. If she was unable to suppress the tears, her father threatened to thrash her until she stopped howling. 'And little Gerda choked back her tears and promised: "I'll be good. I won't cry any more if you love me"'[1].

That sentence: 'I'll be good if you love me' is the motive for relationships between many of the unloved. It is important for them to find personal expression – in short, easily remembered sentences, which they can repeat to themselves in critical situations – for their individual motivation within relationships.

In earlier times, this second unloved game, 'So that you love me', was played by considerably more women than men. Today the number of men who also indulge is growing. Once this game has been completely seen through, the longing for what was missed out on during childhood and adolescence must be sufficiently expressed in one's present existence so that the past can still be made good through the capacity to get one's way and assert oneself. Improvisation, pleasure in spontaneous ideas, and wit help there. When I am together with such people, I sometimes notice that I get listless and tired, which is how they almost always experience life. But how wonderful then is their awakening to lightness, lack of premeditation, and free flow!

'I LOVE YOU – LOVE ME TOO!'

The leitmotif for the third unloved game is *I love you – love me too!* The protagonist's liking for someone also contains a concealed aggressive demand that the other should return this love – now and unmistakeably. The partner feels pressurised and increasingly disinclined to do so. Now the dramatic phase in such relationships gets under way. An intensive look saying: 'Love me! After all, I love you!' is accompanied by the tragic regard of the unrequited. The intermingling of the two gazes produces annoyance. In this unloved game the second phase is also the most intensive since it too brings together what is yearned for: the partner's love – accompanied by the trauma of internalised withholding of love by one of the parents. Someone trapped in this game wants to awaken the other's love, but in reality his lack of freedom drives the partner away. The two opposing strivings become clearly apparent in this contradiction. The powerfully proclaimed demand for love makes the partner feel like an incapable child, unable to meet the other's wishes. As children break away from parents more violently if the latter demand their love, so too a partner begins to detach him- or herself if compulsively commanded to love. If the person concerned enjoyed a good upbringing, he or she displays consideration. But this politeness isn't acknowledged, so ever greater ruthlessness seems unavoidable – no matter how good the upbringing may have been – in order to get away from the other. The catastrophe is complete. The destiny of a daughter inadequately loved by her father, or a son by his mother, fulfils itself yet again. Those close to the unrequited are then made to feel the tragedy of what has happened. The unrequited experience a sense of lonely grandeur, whereas the world around sometimes sees them as drab characters.

'I DON'T BELIEVE YOU LOVE ME'

The fourth unloved game, the last in this chapter, is completely different and yet related: *'I don't believe you love me'*. This a hidden challenge. Guilt feelings are awoken, and saviour instincts activated. Protagonists in this fourth unloved game usually select partners who themselves constantly feel they somehow never meet life's demands.

A woman with the suppressed reproach of 'I don't believe you love me' in her eyes inflames the heart of a man who knows her sad, unappeased gaze from his never satisfied mother, who cast a needy eye over her son as well as her husband. At the age of twelve such a son said to his mother: 'Someone else would have treated you better than my father'. The mother blushed happily, regarding her son with sad-eyed gratitude. Surprised by so much intensity, he suddenly didn't know what to do any longer, and didn't feel up to a task that was still unclear to him. And yet that was his first experience of happiness with a woman whom he recognised as a woman. And it was the same confusing torment of love he felt once again when at their first meeting his wife-to-be regarded him with that sad, reproachful look: 'I don't believe you love me'. He wasn't aware at the time that he rapidly took on the role of his father, who was also unable to convince his wife that he loved her – just as the wife was equally unaware that she wanted her boy friend and later husband to be just like the father, who during her childhood used her for his own purposes but did not love her for her own sake. This unloved game makes clear what is also true of all the others. These are games for two or in fact for four since one of each partner's parents plays a part, hidden by the forces of repression.

THREE

'Everyone Loves Me' and Other Unloved Games

The unloved we shall now be considering also lacked 'sufficiently good mothering' (Melanie Klein) or 'fathering'. The first unloved game can be characterised with the demand: *The other should love*. A young woman in analysis with me always demonstrated three phases in the way she encountered me within a cycle of relationship. To begin with she bubbled over with charm and pleasantness, showering me with compliments and furtive promises for the time 'when the analysis is over'. Then even the most cautious of my interpretations led her to feel pressurised, forced into a corner, and completely at my mercy. Finally she sought weaknesses and mistakes in me, devaluing me and attempting to gain power over me.

Her love affairs followed the same course. Driven by yearning for love, she lured a man who was usually her inferior, admired him with all her soul, and transmitted unmistakeable erotic signals until she 'conquered' him, his sexuality ignited, and he insisted that she fulfil her promise. The woman's mood then changed abruptly. She felt pressurised and caught in a hopeless situation, and became as cold and frigid as ice. So first she tempted and then she thwarted. Finally, in order not to doubt herself and despair, she turned the tables, and lost all interest in the man she had succeeded in inflaming. Following Watzlawick's conclusion: 'There's something wrong with anyone who loves me'[1], she calls him a ridiculous dwarf with whom she can't be bothered.

Since the second phase of distress and the third of devaluation were by no means pleasant for her, she learnt to

increasingly prolong the initial period of furtive suspenseful eroticism and veiled seduction. She would have liked
to make that into a permanent state of affairs. Most of all
she would have liked to spend her life on the border-line
leading to a dubious paradise, just before the point where
billowing yearning erupted into banal fulfilment, awaiting
and obstructing relaxation of tension with breath held.

Analysis provided the ideal setting for her unloved games.
The rules of analysis forbade what bad experience had led her
not to want anyway, namely sexual relations, and permitted
the excitement of pulsating eroticism held in check, which
she did want. Only one thing did not occur, and that was
everything for her: 'The other should love', relieving her of
the burden of loving, making her forget that she herself could
not love. Because that one thing was lacking – because I was
not ready to play along in her unloved game – everything was
called into question. She wondered whether I was the right
analyst for her, and whether her game might be absolutely
right seeing that the fundamental nature of human existence involved nothing but travelling, being underway, and
new departures, a moment of relaxation between time and
eternity, between 'already' and 'not yet', merely a promise
without fulfilment. Only later did she discover that love is
'tranquillity in movement', and receptivity to another person's love through yielding oneself.

First, however, the hidden partner in her unloved games
had to be accompanied out of the cellar onto the ground
floor: her father who loved her too much and thus didn't
really love her, who pressurised her sexually, playing her
off against the mother, and stimulating the unholy love of
incest whilst simultaneously intensifying her defensiveness.
He was 'the other who loved', whose 'love' provoked her
feelings of powerlessness. As long as she went along with
rather than uncovering his wicked game, still loving him as
the only one to the point of death and beyond, other men,
her partners, had to vicariously tolerate what she could not
do to her father: unmasking, devaluing, and taking him off
his pedestal.

She herself said: 'I have men love me' – long before the
popular book presenting a contrary, generalised perspective
appeared (*Men have themselves loved*[2]). Having oneself loved

instead of loving and being loved occurs among women and men as a result of the powerlessness caused by early subjugation. Since the partner is then expected to love for both, he (or she) never loves enough. He is constantly tested as to whether he loves everything about the other inclusive of lack of love, whether he is ready for ever renewed sacrifice and renunciation, and whether he persists even when rejected or chased away. Since the partner simultaneously loves both too little and too much, this unloved game completely paralyses both. The princess is ultimately herself the victim of the trials she imposes on the would-be prince.

'YOU NEVER LOVE ME ENOUGH'

That leads to the next unloved game: *You never love me enough*. Like all the other unloved games, this also contains a grain of truth – but concealed in a place inaccessible to the protagonist. If we comprehend love, so to speak, extensively – love of all the details constituting the other's personality, from the tips of the toes to the crown of the head, and everything that lies between – it remains an insoluble task which can bring us to despair. Viewed quantitatively it is impossible to love someone completely. There is too much that is personal, incomprehensible, alien, and unattractive for a single person's love to be able to digest all that. Even if millions were to embrace me, together they could not love everything in me because I am a distinctive mixture of human characteristics, and thus uncomprehended and unloved in many respects.

The perspective is topsy turvy in this game too. A specific man is fixated on what he believes to be his partner's lack of attractiveness, and on the question of whether she rather than all the others is really the right person for him – or whether someone else might perhaps be able to give him more. If he is fixated on what he gets from his girl friend, and lacks feeling for what comes to life in exchanges between them, he must time and again ask whether he is sufficiently loved. The answer is always 'No'. In order to silence that misguided question within himself, he finally altered the perspective, paid more attention to his own stirrings and less to expectations of his girl friend, more to the question of whether he himself loves and less to whether he is himself loved. He gradually starts to understand himself better in connection with his partner. He begins to feel whether and how he loves her in a given situation. He learns that, for instance, by paying attention to the warmth emitted by his body – say, in the right arm when holding his girl friend, or simply when it is close to her without actually touching: whether the arm is warm or cold, and whether it feels good or not. Thanks to such bodily perceptions, he comes closer to himself than was previously the case, begins to experience his own body, and to adopt the perspective of loving or not loving, or at least of someone actively involved.

The task of every real analysis is expansion of one's awareness though relativising what was previously a single perspective. That also entails *body analysis* in terms of inner awareness of body reactions in critical life situations where complexes prevail. This should not be confused with body therapy where the body is guided towards new experiences by way of exercises. Analysis must not be restricted to dreams, daydreams, complexes, or Freudian slips. Body analysis in terms of conscious perception of what autonomously occurs in the body is an invaluable component in any analysis, particularly in the case of people who are fixated on others rather than related to themselves. Well-meaning attentiveness – as opposed to detached self-observation – is thus directed towards one's own body. That makes possible, for instance, dissolution of the remote image of an idealised girl friend. The more directly we perceive our bodily sensations, the less we need remote idealised images. An analyst should therefore not merely investigate his clients' dreams, but must also put such questions as: 'How did your right upper thigh feel when you sat to the left of your boy/girl friend after having just quarrelled?' Such a question only seems strange to people who live in their heads. These remarks anticipate the third part of the book.

'ALWAYS A LITTLE TOO LATE'

Another unloved game is called *'Always a little too late'*. It is generally known that people who often come too late either want to demonstrate their importance; or, feeling unimportant, 'want' to delay being a burden to others for as long as possible, which is ultimately the same; or 'want' to express indifference or even contempt for the person waiting. I put the verb 'want' in inverted commas because unloved games are always unconscious, spontaneous processes, and never maliciously intended. I am concerned here with de-piction of a more subtle, serious 'late-coming', which can happen several times on the same day, making impossible direct emotional contact. All the unloved suffer from that. This unloved game thus always involves one or several others. The speed with which it occurs should not mislead about its significance. I am talking about what often only entails a delay of seconds in eye contact.

Let's assume that a man walking along the street sees a woman whom he immediately thinks sympathetic. He looks at her briefly, she also looks at him. Then he immediately looks away, perhaps even before their eyes meet. He feels overwhelmed by so much sudden closeness. He pulls himself together, and looks again in the hope that the woman has not yet turned away. Even if she hasn't done so, his look still contains the fright of just previously. It has become fixed and glassy. The man would like to establish contact with his look, but his eye has become a window pane against which the woman's glance collides like a bird, falling dead to the ground. Or, in a less serious case, his eye is not altogether a defensive mirror, but also, to some slight degree, an organ of contact – yet inner doubt does not permit sufficient light to stream out into freedom. His eye still courageously flickers for a while. Then it becomes lifeless, and an opportunity for encounterr has been lost.

Of course, such slightly out-of-sync *encounters*, which be-come *'mis-encounters'* (Martin Buber), do not merely occur with strangers. They are particularly painful when involving the people we most care about. The person concerned scarcely notices our love, desperately seeking expression – or at least less than our defensiveness, which is interpreted as hostility, giving rise to a brusque, aggressive, cold, or hurt response. These are generally fleeting, casual processes, so they do not even cross the threshhold of consciousness. But the mood has changed, and the person concerned does not know why. Many times on the same day he becomes inexplicably restless, 25 despondent, depressed, as if he had missed out on something. And he really has too. He always misses the same thing: the liberating encounter where his energy could spring up and establish contact with the world. Much has already been gained if this brief process becomes conscious. Here too the large is contained in the small. A partnership also consists of nothing but such *brief processes and momentary movements*. Those therefore have to be perceived, understood, sensed, and liberated. Appropriate *mini-analyses* are often much more important than analyses of the greater context[3]. Both of course belong together, but if we restrict ourselves to the latter the large-scale insights fail us in the lesser practicalities of the present moment. Anyone who always only wants what is most important obstructs the smallest things and the whole.

'I'LL BUY YOU'

Let's move on to another unloved game. Its main theme is: *I'll buy you*. The unloved attracted by this game come from families where there was more money than love – or, more generally, where money had the symbolic value of love. Money represented love. The parents attempted to compensate for incapacity to give their children love with money, which they distributed in doses or withheld according to whether their offspring accorded with expectations or not. Money thus attained the significance of love for these children. After the parent's death, money again turns out to be the highest family value when the estate is divided up. A multi millionaire thus took his brother to court over less than a thousand Swiss Francs. At issue there was not the money but a demonstration that 'I'm getting more love from my parents than you'.

If money has taken on this symbolic significance, any love becomes something that is purchaseable. 'If I give you a car, I love you' runs the logic of this well-regarded form of prostituted relationship. Or the other way around: 'I give you money so you must love me', an expectation often also applied to the therapist. The children of families where love is for sale react by stealing things if the parents show preference for a brother or sister. They thus grab for what is not given them voluntarily – for love. The same children give presents to class mates whose liking they want to gain. Money is a means of payment even for love.

Such misdirected love is fatal, hindering the development of psychological paths where love can move freely, able to open up into life. People with the motto 'I'll buy you' are clumsy in all other demonstrations of love except for giving money. It's obvious that such people are easily exploited – by those who believe that 'You should love, not me'. They thus fill bottomless barrels, and do not succeed in quenching their own thirst. Businessmen often tend to play the 'I'll buy you' game in their marriage, and recompense themselves in their business practices. A game against love in every respect with money instead of love, and having instead of being.

And yet it is usually sensitive people in need of love, who play the 'I'll buy you' game. An affluent man thus several times fell in love with young women in need, whom he assisted with money by financing their studies in order to gain their affection – but without being aware of his motives. This game was, however, one-sided. Each time the young woman in question failed to share his unconscious precondition that money should be reciprocated with love – without further ado. In fact once she had the money, she sought love, but with another man. So long as the misalliance of money and love persists, the person concerned will miss out on love.

'EVERYONE LOVES ME'

The inventiveness of love that has gone astray in unloved games is infinite, demonstrating that love is a great demon as Diotima told Socrates: the indispensable power that holds our life together, which we unceasingly seek, even in roundabout and misguided ways. So I shall arbitrarily break off this series, which could be continued for long, with a final unloved game. This involves the terse and gratifying pronouncement: *Everyone loves me.*

That little sentence often ends with a slightly raised voice, as if with a comma instead of full stop, and as if it must continue, which it should. Only four words are missing. Those would immediately betray the unloved game. The complete sentence runs: 'Everyone loves me except for one person'. This one person, who does not love the speaker, was initially the father or the mother, then the partner, or the business friend, or someone who didn't invite me, or the secretary demanding a rise in pay, or the apprentice who leaves work ten minutes early, or the boss who failed to say 'Good morning' today, or the daughter who wants more pocket money. For the person whom everyone loves, withdrawal of love is an ever-present threat, often in the case of the very person whose love now seems most necessary. 'Everyone loves me', yet the one person who really counts now does not. That little sentence is an ineffective attempt at dealing with a permanent hurt. Everyone really does love me, so how can this one person, who to his own misfortune happens not to love me, upset me in any way? My wife is ultimately not the world; nor is my boss, my business friend, someone who didn't invite me, another person who didn't want to go to the cinema with me, my son who came later than agreed yesterday, the worker who sent me an excessive bill, the school friend who forgot my birthday for the first time – just this one person doesn't love me. But everyone else loves me. Isn't that splendid?

People who are much loved need love like children – and as children they lacked love, which accounts for their constantly wounded feelings. The much-loved were deprived. They missed their parents, perhaps because these parents made love dependent on good behaviour. 'I do love you' – such a father may have said 'but you mustn't disturb me or else I won't love you any longer'. And the child did disturb its father and love was withdrawn by this strong personality – in contrast to the child who in that situation 'chooses' the 'So that you love me' unloved game. The outcome is that the adult, who as a child forfeited love, seeks love throughout his life. Everyone must love him or her: the postman, the cleaning woman, the girl at the telephone exchange, the boss to whom he has just handed in notice, and the woman he divorced. The much-loved person is voracious. If all attempts at being loved more come to nothing, one's partner must ultimately suffer. Does she love me today? Didn't she just give me a cool and curt 'Good morning'? And wasn't she tired yesterday evening? The much-loved person must be much loved, and in the long term that is exhausting for the partner. This partner seeks peace, becomes remote and cuts herself off, and becomes the only person who doesn't love the much-loved man. And the old song of the unloved is played through yet again.

This is the way of suffering facing all the unloved just because they cannot give expression with body and soul to a single sentence: 'My father didn't love me', 'My mother didn't love me', or 'My father and mother didn't love me' – thereby exorcising and overcoming this trauma once and for all.

FOUR

Psycho-Energetics

1. CONCEPT AND EXPERIENCE OF LIFE-ENERGY

How does it come about that I have long been tracking down psycho-energetics without initially naming it as such? What lies behind the fascination with flow, rhythm, movement that unites, and equilibrium within immediately experienced vitality? I'll suggest an answer by way of four stories from my childhood and adolescence.

I still remember exactly how, at the age of perhaps seven, I went barefoot home for lunch after school one hot summer day. The air shimmered over the freshly tarred, black road, which yielded softly to my feet. I recollect the great stillness and the dizzying vibrations of the heated air. All of a sudden a feeling of ardent joy flooded me. This was more than happiness. It was the most profound realism possible. I stood transfixed, enjoying to the full the sweet shudders that rushed through my body. It was as if a fine electrical rain were running through me. I paused, together with the sun now at its zenith. For the first time in my life, my limited everyday existence, my parents, school, paled into insignificance. A vibratory relationship with the world was established. I was nothing but this relationship, linked in the great here and now with the whole. Ever since that time I love the smell of hot tar, stopping wherever a street is being repaired.

Some years later – I must have been thirteen at the time – I sat with my older sister and another girl in the town hall at Winterthur, my birthplace, attending the rehearsal for a concert. I had gone there without any great interest, in fact only so as to be together with the two girls. Reger's variations on Mozart's A major sonata were played. And suddenly it was there. Today I would say that I became the music's sounding board through and through. Shudders of delight and terror rushed through me; I became dizzy; my entire body shivered and shook – and I was afraid the girls on my right would notice. This spontaneous experience of energy was the most intensive of my life. In front of me to the left was a pillar. I pressed myself firmly against it so as to stop my trembling. But at the same time I felt myself unimaginably free and flowing as never before. The secret underlying the world seemed to be opening up to me. It was only twenty five years later that I told this story to anyone – to Heike, my wife, at a period when this experience of energy still occurred from time to time, less ecstatically but more prolonged, warming life as a whole and starting to transform it. In later concerts I several times sought out the pillar against which I had pressed, but the energy never happened there again. The search for 'places of power' can entail flight from the only location where such things can occur – in one's own life.

At the age of eighteen I had a similar experience while staying in Florence, providing coaching for a school friend. I went by scooter, borrowed from a neighbour's daughter, to Assisi, and then walked to Eremo dei Carceri. I sat beyond the chapel in an olive grove offering an expansive view of the plain. Once again it was midday, the hour of the goat-hoofed shepherd Pan. The leaves of the olive trees rustled dryly in a fast rhythm, too quick to be followed. The air hummed with heat. A tense silence prevailed. And suddenly all that and I myself were a single great event, woven out of self-perpetuating intensities. I didn't know what was happening to me, and wept with a sense of liberation. At that time I decided to become a Catholic priest, but by binding myself in established structures in order to attain the 'great liberation' I lost it.

Nevertheless, during the eight years I was a priest there were also occasions when I experienced life-energy very directly. That happened within the church realm from time to time – for instance during saying the rosary with its monotonous succession of unchanging phrases incorporating a five-stage inner experience. But it also sometimes occurred in moments of friendship – as in the following story.

On a warm summer evening I was sitting in front of the

Bremgarten studio of Heidi Widmer, a Swiss artist with whom I've been friends for twenty five years. This studio was at the top of a steep slope above a sharp bend in the river Reuss, which was not dammed at that time. Heidi was just back from two years in South America, and we were celebrating the reunion. She cooked an improvised Sicilian meal. After eating we fell silent. The river rippled beneath us. The water glittered darkly. All of a sudden it was there, an enchantment leading to something totally self-evident which, so long as we are in it, seems unable to come to an end because we are totally identical with ourselves. Our breathing, the lazy motion of the waves, the delight-inducing, splashing, murmuring sounds, the shimmering reflections of lights in the moving river, and persistent traces of the aroma of our meal all united in a single rhythm, comprising those elements and much besides, in a fundamental wave of being. Life was without questions, and the ego was delivered from itself.

Only after undergoing dark and difficult moments did I grasp that such experiences of life-energy within existence do not change anything, except perhaps for transforming themselves into a new, fundamental sense of life permeating our least actions and thoughts. When I comprehended that, the idea of *psycho-energetics* as a thread guiding through psychotherapy surfaced. I remembered Teilhard de Chardin's call – in a paper presented to French psychoanalysts after world war II – for 'elaboration of Energetics (psycho-energetics)'. So far as I know, Teilhard only used the expression psycho-energetics this one time, and I have taken it over from him.

The Concept of Life-Energy

What do I understand the psychological concept of *life-energy* to mean? This differs from the physical concept of energy and such manifestations as electricity, gravity, or thermal radiation. The expression life-energy is based on generally known, verifiable, and related experiences. I mention eight such experiences. Firstly, the life-energy to be experienced in *drive, impetus,* and *acceleration*: that is to say, the experience of 'zest' in human existence –

Piaget's *'élan'*, Bergson's *'élan vital'*, and Jung's *'energy-gradient'*. Secondly, the experience of pulsating *tension* and *relaxation, charging* and *discharging,* and thus of *ordering rhythm.* Thirdly, the experience of *polar tension* in conscious endurance of psychological opposites – *polar consciousness.* Fourthly, the experience of *blocking* or *disruption* of life-energy in psychological complexes and bodily tensions. Fifthly, the experience of *the starting up again of the energy flow,* that is, the transition from immobility to power. Sixthly, the experience of *resonance* – *'attunement': sounding, echoing,* and *harmonious vibration.* Seventh, the experience of increased energy through consciously allowing *self-regulation* within the individual organism and in relationships. And eighth, the experience of *union with the cosmos.* It would be better to speak of *eight variants of a single experience of energy* rather than eight experiences. They all have in common subjectively experienced *intensity.* I shall discuss each of them in greater detail in the appropriate place.

The definition of psycho-energetics is based on experiencing energy. **Psycho-energetics involves access by way of depth psychology to energy as the basic experience within existence, dissolving inhibitions and creating the precondition for spiritual growth**. It subjects analysis of the contents of a person's childhood memories, of the current life situation, and symbolically expressed future potential to the common criterion of whether life is enhanced or obstructed. It promotes that *sensitivity to the strongest emotion,* which should be followed at a given moment, *and responsiveness to bodily expression of the psyche.* It sets love free – the relationship to you, the world, and the self, felt and implemented in gestures of affirmation. This definition will also become clearer in what follows.

Energy is always lacking when someone feels unloved. If a schoolboy is convinced he's no good at maths because his father was an excellent mathematician but despised by his wife, sharing everything in common with her inclusive of contempt for the man, he feels paralysed, washed out, and incapable in maths lessons – lacking energy. The reluctant maths pupil cannot as yet hit on the idea that behind his frustration over mathematics ultimately lies his mother's lack of love for her husband.

Energy is what is experienced in activity, in performance, *at work*. The word is derived from the Ancient Greek *energeia*, which literally translated means 'at work'. The substantive *'ergon'* is linguistically related to our 'work'. Energeia was a word newly coined by Aristotle, the Greek philosopher, and means whatever *'works'* in terms of *making* and *being effective*. In German, the etymological origins of reality (*Wirklichkeit*) – in the sense of something that works – also entail energy and execution of a movement, as opposed to *'dynamis'*, the word Aristotle used to characterise still idle potentiality.

Defining Life-Energy

Even though the impact of life-energy can be described, the phenomenon itself cannot be defined and is nowhere to be found except 'at work' and in action, fulfilling life and being. Attempts at definition have nevertheless been made time and again. The human mind has difficulty in refraining from circumscribing mobile experience without limits. Sigmund Freud himself for a long time hesitated over whether he should view the libido, hitherto viewed sexually, as being instead one of many manifestations of energy. His vacillation is probably to be explained in terms of the influence exerted by Carl Gustav Jung, who upheld the latter view in his *Symbols of Transformation* (1912). 'If we penetrate further and deeper', wrote Freud in 1914, 'we may discover that sexual energy, the libido, is only a variant of an *energy generally operational in the brain* . . . something that is capable of intensification, diminution, displacement, and discharge, expanding along the tracks of memory of an idea like an electrical charge across the surface of a body'.[2] We know that Freud subsequently distanced himself from this assumption of a general life-energy, restricting his concept of the libido to sexuality. Only later did he consider the possibility of a more comprehensive understanding of the libido, but that does not concern us here.

The most appropriate symbol for energy is also the oldest: *Fire*, 'eternal fire'. In the Western cultural sphere this was disseminated by Heraclitus. Attempts at making energy into a kind of substance, something graspable and com-prehensible, such as characterising life-energy as a universal aura within magnetism, or ether in the natural sciences up to the start of the twentieth century, seem to have been unaware of its symbolic character. Michelson's experiment and Einstein's theories finally led to rejection of the assumption of such a mysterious 'energy substance' as ether. It seems to me that the reification of life-energy is made unnecessary by our seeing humanity and the universe as a whole, as an extended organism where all processes are associated in an inner connection and order. A mysterious, universal, freely moving substance is thus replaced by the natural interrelationship between all processes.

With regard to the human organism, life-energy does not entail something in addition to circulation of the blood and hormones, sexual and electrical charge and discharge, contraction and relaxation of the muscles, metabolism, the flow of thoughts, and so on. But why is the general term 'energy' used for that, both within esotericism and in everyday speech, when we say: 'I've no energy'?

The word life-energy derives from *unified* perception of all the many diverse processes within the organism as a *whole*. It thus reflects the interrelationship and connection between all life processes within the entire organism. It reveals that the whole of our life is not identical with the sum of its parts, and that life constitutes a functioning, self-regulating unity. *Life-energy* is dynamic *experiencing of the whole* (see the seventh experience of life-energy).

Another question comes to mind. Why does esotericism, which has become more widely accessible in recent years, view life-energy as a cosmic phenomenon rather than something limited to the individual organism? The answer lies in experiences such as the following. If I'm in a state of relaxed concentration and attentiveness, and gently link my hands, held vertically, with another person's hands, I have the physical feeling that energy is flowing into, through, and out of me. Energy seems to be able to flow in and out of me through these warmed-up hands. Such an intensive experience of extensive energy circulation is not dependent on sexual encounters or direct contact. It has always been accessible through poetic, non-rational language too. That is also to be experienced in nature – on the seashore or under the stars – and not just with other human beings. All the things of this world are vitally connected within a single energy field. How can we doubt that when we ourselves experience it so vibrantly?

But what do we really experience? We experience that our life-processes are activated to the degree that we are intensively related to the world around us. That is a fundamental truth of human existence and human development at all ages, from the small child to the old person. Realised relationship is the central factor in development. To that extent we really can speak of a general circulation of energy. But to conclude from this that life-energy is a mysterious, universal, freely moving 'vitalising substance', beyond the elements composing our organisms, does not accord with scientific reality. That is the outcome of an experiential language which, like all such languages, does not differentiate between perception and significance, event and insight. This metaphorical view of life-energy is, so to speak, a materialised perception, today causing a great deal of confusion within use of the word. The relationship to the cosmos really is the precondition for our vitalisation – but in terms of the fact that the individual potential within a person is awoken alongside increasing awareness of 'being in the world'. There is also no doubt that individual life-potential is archetypal in character – that is to say, its dynamics are identical with another person's life potential. And yet this life-energy is not some cosmic 'Flow' that we merely need to tap in order to become more vital. Such a view would be questionable for a psychotherapist, promoting inflation of the ego, neglect of banal everyday things such as issues within relationships, and false solutions of problems by way of strokes of genius. It is certainly important to stress the receptive dimension of consciousness and relevant insights. I myself have often done so. But that entails active readiness for reception, not an infantile attitude of expectation.

In the modern debate about the essential nature of life-energy, it is interesting how the old extreme positions within Christian theology with reference to the relationship between nature and grace have reappeared in new clothing. The 'flow of grace' is not in addition to nature or anything supernatural, but entails human vitalisation following an opening to outer impulses and energy inputs. As recently as the fifties, Pope Pius XII revoked the professorship of Henri de Lubac, a French Jesuit for whom I wrote my theological doctorate in 1968 and today a cardinal, because, *mutatis mutandis*, he had represented such views in his book *Le Surnaturel*. Conversely, today's esoteric literature often represents a position similar to that still to be found in conservative Catholic and pietistic Protestant theology.

Freely accessible life-energy corresponds to the ancient children's dream of the all-providing mother, the land where milk and honey flow. The dream itself is important and fruitful since it stimulates our feeling, thinking, and actions. But materialisation of the dream in the idea of an omnipresent elixir of life which we only need discover in order to be healed and saved belongs to the domain of magic. The Romantic Age knew that temptation. Magic obstructs what the dream intends: vitalisation of the drive towards development. New feelings should not lead us to forget thinking, or else we will think against ourselves.

Mystical Experience

The concept of life-energy possesses a power that can explode systems since it doesn't allow itself to be identified with any partial human process, or any specific instinct such as sexuality or aggression. The only criterion for activation of life-energy is that something 'works', whatever that 'something' may be. A psychotherapy that ultimately only aims at life becoming real in clients constantly calls conventions and set thought-patterns into question. A mounting sense of what is 'at work' within ourselves provides a freedom which not even the most complete psychological system or school of depth psychology can provide. At its most profound level the experience of energy is *mystical*. The mystical explodes frozen ideas that have become systems— through experiencing movements and phenomena transcending such effects. The 'real human being'—as Meister Eckhart calls him—lives out of a mysticism where views about life are superseded by life itself at every moment.

> Someone may question life for a thousand years: why are you alive? It would answer if it could speak: 'I live because I live'. That is because

life lives out of its own ground and is its own
source. So it lives out of itself without asking why.
If someone asks a real human being, acting out of
his own ground: why do you do what you do? – he
would say, if he answers similarly: 'I act because I
act'.[3]

2.   MAGNETISM AND PSYCHO-ENERGETICS

Healing through Relationship

In his book '*Der Zauberbaum*' ('The Magic Tree'), an epic essay
on the origins of psychoanalysis in *magnetism* or mesmerism,
Peter Sloterdijk has the young Viennese doctor Jan van
Leyden write in a letter: 'Instead of calmly reflecting on man's
inner structures, I have been dragged into this inner realm
where everything is in a state of exciting flux rather than
there being any trace of tranquillity'.[4] He also speaks of the
surmounting of 'rigid local identities' in favour of a universal
'subject in flux'.[5] Beneath the irony the reader senses the
author's passion for his hero's search for barrier-bursting
pleasure in the individual's energy-based union with the
world. And that is the core experience of magnetism, the
precursor of depth psychology at the end of the eighteenth
century.

   In order to make what follows more comprehensible,
I'll provide some information about *magnetism*[6] here. Its
originator, Franz Anton Mesmer (1734–1814), a doctor, was
dissatisfied with mechanistic medicine, which only repairs
individual parts of the patient. He recognised the psychological factor involved in illness, and saw the patient's *will to
health* as the most important aspect of healing. Magnetism
endeavoured to counter the illness's 'resistance' by setting
in motion the sick person's *vital principle*, founded on the
'*healing power of the community*'. That could only unfold if
'the ego which wants to want' stands down[7]. Mesmer offered
'group therapy' even at that time. The patients formed a
'*magnetic chain*' so as to strengthen the energy flow, the
'aura', in contact with others and in the community. This
'aura' entailed a '*reciprocal influencing*' which, according to
Mesmer, 'prevails among heavenly bodies, the earth, and

animal bodies'. For Mesmer this 'reciprocal influencing' was an 'active relationship' (interaction) operating through 'magnetic inclination' towards the opposite pole. The same is also true within the individual body. I stress that the word *inclination* has overtones of *love*. Love is thus the essential element within this mysterious aura. Mesmer was initially of the opinion that healing derived from magnetising objects. Hence the name magnetism. Soon, however, he discovered that the healing inflow came from himself. From that time onwards he called his healing method 'animal magnetism', based on curative vital attraction. For the 'magnetist' there was, however, a danger of magically overestimating his own healing power instead of attributing it to the power of the community.

Apart from cases of hysteria, Mesmer treated people who were physically very ill, strengthening their will to health so that some of these patients were also healed.

'Animal magnetism' – as Mesmer wrote – causes within the human body 'a kind of ebb and flow' – relaxation and tension, discharge and charge, expansion and concentration. The task is to intensify this natural movement. This is where Mesmer's celebrated *'crisis theory'* operates. Healing takes place by way of 'crises and perceptible discharges in accordance with the nature of the illnesses involved'.[8] Deploying the previously mentioned chain formation in both 'group' and 'individual' therapy – primarily by way of moving the hands just above the patient's body from top to bottom, or a laying on of hands, or putting pressure on painful places[9] – the magnetist physically achieves the opening of 'occlusions' (blockages) and what Alfred Adler called *sense of community*. This increases the individual's energy level, and super-intensification of symptoms of illness gets the life-process going. Otherwise scarcely noticeable bodily rhythms and vibrations intensify through resonance to the point of spasmic twitches and convulsions. As soon as Mesmer held his open hand at a suitable distance over the forehead, breast, or stomach, a 'transfer' occurred, expressing itself as a cluster of vibrations. This signified that the *entire organism* – rather than a single organ – was reacting. For Mesmer the *whole human being was the subject of healing*. A sick organ was only healed as part of a whole. The 'pricking sensation' of the first vibration could become violent, spontaneous movements of the body. Sorrowful laments turned into intense screams. The sick person's state seemed to get worse until he finally moved convulsively several times and then broke down ('défaillance'). The symptoms of illness had triumphed and could therefore vanish[10]. The crisis was the healing.

Mesmer himself did not then know that he was pursuing psychotherapy rather than organic medicine. But do we know exactly what we are doing? Doesn't the psychotherapist, concerned with 'animal' magnetism, sometimes achieve astonishing successes with his clients' bodily ailments even though it can hardly be proved that such healing resulted from treatment? Sometimes, however, that can be demonstrated. At an American congress of doctors in 1987, it was statistically established that the HIV positive patients undergoing psychotherapy warded off Aids for significantly longer than those who received no psychological treatment.

In the mid-nineteenth century, Carl Gustav Carus realised that Mesmer had practised psychotherapy, and that it was the *'rapport'*, the relationship between magnetist and patient focusing on the latter's *unconscious*, which brought about healing.[11] Carus was the first person to speak of the unconscious in psychological terms, attributing magnetic significance to it. The impact of the therapist on the patient's unconscious involves an *energy process* as a consequence of inclination, of liking, between the two. But that primary significance of psychotherapy as psycho-energetics increasingly declined in importance as a result of mounting specialisation and structuring.

Mesmer healed through interrelationship rather than pursuing body therapy as the term is understood today. He himself touched a patient very little. Occasional contact was a sign of his physical presence and not manipulation. It was a bodily impulse, which can also be given without contact – simply through showing warm *concern* and real, conscious *participation* in the other's life. Such concern includes resonance and empathy. That is the essential element in the relationship between the therapist, attending to energetic processes, and his client. Physical contact need not, however, be avoided at all costs. A stronger handshake or an embrace after a particularly intensive session make a client more free rather than more dependent.

The magnetists exerted great influence on nineteenth century philosophy. Schelling wrote of 'magnetic and electrical manifestations' in both nature and the human consciousness – 'the dynamic process resulting from the attraction and repulsion of like and unlike poles'.[12] Schopenhauer even prophesied in 1850: 'A time will come when philosophy, animal magnetism, and natural science, making unprecedented progress in all its aspects, will throw a bright light on one another, revealing truths man cannot hope to attain in any other way'.[13]

The concept of energy may perhaps lead the reader to think of Freud's *pleasure principle*. What the two have in common is affirmation of emotionality. The difference is that the energy principle is not countered by any so-called reality principle. The relationship with a human being's *entire* reality, inclusive of grief-stricken life conditions and such emotions as fear, rage, and sadness, mobilises life-energy.

Energy Principle

The way out of unfavourable and even destructive circumstances entails therapeutically experiencing what is involved (Perls). Only in that way can a turning-point be attained within the 'magnetic' or energy 'crisis'. The *energy principle* accords with a profound, comprehensive sense of reality. The human being does not merely seek pleasure and the avoidance of pain, even though it often seems so. He or she also seeks fulfilment of his or her humanity through aggression, sadness, and suffering. 'Negative' emotions are also an expression of our life-force. Someone, for instance, who aggressively parts company with another is thereby perhaps creating the preconditions for new life within a new frame of reference. And isn't the death of an individual a dying into the ongoing life of others, an indication of the relativity of what we call the ego? The separation of the pleasure principle and the reality principle, of Eros and Thanatos, is merely provisional within psycho-energetic thinking, expressing a lack of 'animal', vital relationship with reality. Freud wrote to Pfister that the 'oceanic feeling' Romain Rolland speaks of, the feeling of the unity of all things, was unknown to him and probably pathological. So we can see that psychoanalysis lost something – sensitivity to energy processes and their application. Endeavours by schools of depth psychology to establish structures restricted creative freedom, which is only present in a psychotherapy that is mainly concerned with emotional relationships without, however, forgetting childhood memories and developmental images.

At the time when it arose, magnetism could not develop therapeutically since the Enlightenment, focused on the thinking subject, strongly rejected 'bodily thinking' (Sloterdijk) and everything that could not be captured by reason. Banned from the age's science, magnetism degenerated into charlatanism, fairground magic, and superstitious ideas about healing. Eloquent testimony to that is provided by the literature – also covering today's magnetism. Only a hundred years later did a watered-down form of magnetism become acceptable in depth psychology. One of psycho-energetics' objectives is to liberate the original magnetism from magic, and to bring about its therapeutic effectiveness.

In philosophy Friedrich Nietzsche completed the transition to the body and an energy based concept of truth. For him the body was a 'means of knowledge'. Magnetism and psycho-energetics promote the 'curative descent' into the body. 'At issue in every case is exchanging an unreal completeness in favour of an incompleteness which has the advantage of being real'.[14] We need body analysis alongside the analysis of dreams and transference. There is a simple reason for the fact that depth psychologists have paid so little attention to the body as a 'means of knowledge'. Very few have participated in any course on growth of body awareness alongside their training analysis. I do not, however, know a single analyst who did not expand his working methods after having himself followed the 'curative descent' into the body. Analysts do not need to become body therapists, who primarily operate with physical exercises which can also restrict the free dynamism of what seeks spontaneous expression in life. And yet personal experiences of one or several tried and tested methods for becoming aware of oneself through the body are necessary so as to work psycho-energetically as an analyst.

The objective in any psychotherapy is to further a person's capacity for self-curing. As in homeopathic medicine with its very diluted 'high potency' treatment intended only to provide a mini-impulse towards cure, Mesmer and his pupils for the most part limited themselves to brief, rapid 'strokings' which sometimes do not even touch the patient. A brief 'bodily' word, which the therapist drops into the client's existence, also transmits this 'initiatory impetus'. Some therapists attribute the healing impact of their words to the correctness of what they say or indicate. But that is just what is not true in many cases. The symptoms of people who have undergone two successive courses of therapy can react equally well to the two therapists' differing interpretations of what is basically the problem. If we imagine that a third therapist then unmistakably demonstrated the falsity of his precursors' diagnoses, it would by no means be certain that his 'correct' analysis would exert a more healing impact on the client than his colleagues' 'wrong' explanations. The content of interpretations is less important than the energy transferred from the therapist to the client. Transference primarily occurs as a result of the therapist's unprejudiced, warm attentiveness towards the patient. Of course his 'freely floating attentiveness' (Freud) is also more likely to establish the preconditions for a more appropriate interpretation. And yet I have several times had to admit to myself that something had worked which should not have because it was wrong. It was effective despite being wrong, and the client himself later discovered that – because he knew how to make use of the energy-input he received in the vital relationship with me. That is the essential factor. Psycho-energetics is the main connecting thread within psychotherapy, which must be pursued through all interpretations. It in no way leads to a lack of seriousness in analysis. Quite the contrary. It furthers intuition and thus also the probability of correct insights. The psycho-energetic way of working becomes particularly apparent at decisive developmental intersections and turning-points.

Interpreting Dreams

In his analysis of the unconscious, Carl Gustav Jung introduced the final component. What unfulfilled aspect of the
life-plan, what existential possibility, can be uncovered in a
dream? We put the same question with regard to the body:
what possibility of expression is inhibited there and wants
to free itself? What message is concealed behind a constricted
voice? What light glimmers behind an almost lifeless eye?
What emotion is expressed in a jiggling foot? Sometimes I
put such questions absolutely directly, and it is astonishing
how often there are answers which would otherwise never
be given. Therapists should not have standard answers
for such questions, as sometimes seems to be the case
in bioenergetics. That risk also exists in the analysis of
dreams. The therapist's physical presence results in profound
fellow-feeling for the client. A human being comes physically
closer. And that very fellow-feeling – not just an understanding attitude – links the two and awakens slumbering vital
energy.

Doesn't psycho-energetic treatment involve the same danger as hypnosis in working with *suggestions* and thus achieving only short-lived healing? That risk was, after all, the
reason why Freud turned away from hypnosis and instead
took up analysis of transferences. My answer to that is: if
the therapist is fixated on his own power of suggestion, he
lacks open awareness for the *other person*. When, however,
he is focused on the other, his influence never extends
beyond the previously mentioned input of energy. I am
often very cool and detached when I observe that a client
exists psychologically at my expense even though he could
very well live from his own resources. When he experiences both input and withholding in my behaviour, he
learns to become an autonomous human being, increasingly
less dependent on the impulses provided by another person.

That process is as old as psychoanalysis itself, but it only
becomes really spontaneous and natural if the therapist pays
attention – alongside all the verbalised questions – to expressions of energy in what the patient says: for instance, whether

he, so to speak, hangs onto the analyst's lips, immediately greedily sucking in everything that comes out of his mouth; or whether he lets such impulses simply bounce off him; or whether he is shattered and collapses psychologically when the person opposite falls silent; or whether, in the most favourable case, his attitude indicates that he wants nothing but such impulses – and also increasingly few. If the therapist observes such signals, he will react spontaneously with either restraint or attention. Psycho-energetics thus excludes the implanting of suggestions so far as that is possible. Not even magnetism should simply be equated with utilising suggestibility even though it did ultimately lead to the technique of hypnosis. The magnetist knew nothing at that time about transference in the analytical sense, so he did run the danger of attributing successes to his own magical healing power.

During the early stages of psychoanalysis Freud ascertained that hypnosis does not achieve lasting healing, and towards the end of his life he conceded that pure analysis did not heal either. What must be done is to take over the healing elements and discard the non-healing aspects of both. From hypnosis and suggestion we can take over the therapist's bodily presence and solidarity, but must reject the client's loss of will and dependence since successes based on that are short-lived. From psychoanalysis we keep conscious work with memories and developmental patterns, and their transference to the analyst, but must find fault with the lack of 'fellow-feeling' and body analysis.

Many of the elements involved in psycho-energetics are to be found in Jung including a feeling for human wholeness and incorporation in what alchemy called the 'unus mundus', the *one* world, through observation of spontaneously developing archetypal images. I have therefore been influenced by Jung's depth psychology, but am of the opinion that it should constantly take into account the energy principle so as to be more effective.

Mounting familiarity with the practice of psycho-energetics leads me to increasingly see the contents and structures of feeling and thinking in terms of the theory of knowledge and what Nietzsche called the 'poly-perspectival world'. 'You can only see and understand in perspective. There cannot be a science without preconditions. An interpretive perspective must always first exist'.[15] The primordial images of the soul are also just different perspectives within perception of undefinable life-energy, perspectives of flowing images, ultimately comprehensible only in terms of energy rather than content, which have a preference for specific patterns that reflect and further human development.

I recently saw Peter Brook's film *Meetings with Remarkable Men* describing the search for truth by Gurdjieff, based on the Russian's autobiographical writings of the same name. A friend told me that Gurdjieff was Brook's spiritual teacher for several years. A sentence, spoken by a Sufi master, took both my ears and heart by surprise: 'You must change nothing or everything'. I had previously only known 'all or nothing' as a narcissistic reaction on the part of people lacking nuances and powers of discrimination. Was I – in being so moved by this terse challenge – perhaps myself the victim of a childish all embracing demand? But then I recalled those moments of most intensive living – my experiences of life-energy. Wasn't 'nothing or all' also to be found there? Then I reformulated the Sufi master's sentence: 'You must change nothing or the whole of your life'. That seemed meaningful to me. The mystical experience of life-energy is an experience of the whole, not of individual parts. Those by no means become indistinct, but rather appear in a state of mutual order within their reality of relationship. We then see all details afresh, as if by way of an inner light, bound into a whole. They all constitute the whole. I thus gained access to the original formulation of "nothing or everything". The nothing comes first – unlike in the case of a child who first has everything in terms of union with the mother.

Deployment of energy in psychotherapy changes everything even though it adds nothing new in terms of content. In that it is like water whose course adapts to the landscape without adding anything. And yet what would the many be without relationship in the one? What would analysis of childhood memories, dreams, complexes, and developmental images be without the love that unites everything in a single movement?

PART TWO

Understanding

FIVE

Love of Outcasts

In the first part I attempted to awaken capacity for perception of the psychological wound caused by lack of love, to uncover unloved games, and to present psycho-energetics as a guideline within therapy for the unloved. This second part of the book is concerned with intellectual comprehension of the psychological wound from which the unloved suffer. Understanding will bring us to a dividing-line: knowledge does not by itself heal. Nonetheless it is necessary since it makes people more conscious of their suffering, and opens the way towards the crisis that will finally lead to liberation from such affliction. In the fifth chapter we shall investigate feelings of being rejected, in the sixth an adult's childish need for belated parental love, in the seventh depression as an opportunity for liberation from dependences. In the eighth chapter, devoted to discussion of the question of identity, we encounter longing as a basic human experience, which can explain the feeling of not being loved even when sad circumstances are absent.

The unloved are ambivalent about social outcasts because they themselves have been rejected. Such people make them shudder, and yet provoke a secret love. This chapter aims at making that love more conscious, strengthening it through clarification. Love of outcasts is the condition of love of self, which is what the unloved lack.

There was an orphan in my primary school class. He was nondescript and shy, wore long woollen stockings and dark pullovers stinking of moth balls, and blinked uncontrollably. Sometimes I couldn't tear my gaze from him, despite the unpleasantness of his appearance. Unlike him I came from a respected family – about which I was very conceited – and was well clothed. Something burned in me when I looked at this orphan. Today I know that it was the wound of the unloved. If he was punished, I also felt caught out and guilty. Deep within me was someone who was, and wanted to be, an orphan. I longed to reveal this orphan in myself, and yet I was afraid.

One day the teacher gave me some extra work as a punishment, and I was supposed to get my father to append his signature. I forged that signature so as not to displease him. The teacher noticed that immediately, and then uttered words which branded me like a life-long stigma: 'Now you're not worth any more than that boy over there', meaning the orphan. Never again have words provoked so much shame in me. I was ashamed that my social conceit thus disintegrated, but I was mainly ashamed for the orphan. In my confusion I felt that a great injustice had been done to him. At the same time an injustice, beyond reputation and name, was also being done to me. The undisputed assumption behind those terrible words was that the orphan was worth little, and was unloved. I found it almost unbearable that this had now been said so openly. I vaguely sensed that 'if the teacher only loves me as long as I, unlike the orphan, fit in and am respected, he does not love me'. From that day onwards, both at school and at home, I was churned up by the thought of being unloved, an orphan, contrary to all appearances.

I had a similar experience shortly afterwards during the religious instruction given every Saturday midday in preparation for my first communion. The dean asked whether we children could give examples of courage of our Christian convictions. I put up my hand and enthusiastically told how I openly carried my hymn book on the way to church even though subject to the mockery of my Protestant comrades. The dean praised my courage beyond measure. I was, after all, an altar boy and my maternal grandfather had headed the local church community. Three weeks later the dean asked the same question, having probably forgotten that he had already done so. Another boy, the illegitimate child of a poor mother who was always somewhat of an outsider, jumped up and gave the same response as I had. He obviously longed for the recognition that was given me. The dean strode to the back row where the boy sat and slapped him for giving such a stupid answer. Once again the wound of the unloved burnt in me, and I was ashamed for the same reasons as at school.

This time, however, there was also something else. I began to experience myself as being unreal. If praised, I had the feeling: 'That's nothing to do with me. It's only because you're your parents' son, or because you're Catholic, or because you look sympathetic'. Even over twenty years later, when as a young priest I stood up on Sunday mornings to preach in Munich's Ludwigskirche, I sometimes had the feeling: 'If you weren't a priest, no one would listen to you. The approval expressed by people at the service is evoked by the office, not by you. You'd be nothing without that office'. Or: 'Your listeners are caught up in the same illusion as you. Their positive reaction doesn't mean anything'. Only when I stopped working as a priest did this anxiety-engendering feeling vanish, never to return. The certainty of being liked for fortuitous reasons rather than loved for what we really are plagues the unloved. That conceals a profound truth, which no one can avoid over the longer term. But this truth only inhibits development if we really aren't sufficiently loved.

Another species of outcasts preoccupied me too: the naughty, the cheeky, and the bold. I was enormously attracted by the pretty, black-haired son of a foreign worker, who was not afraid of death, the devil, and certainly not our teacher; or the son of a woman railway worker with whom I always smoked cigarettes in hidden corners after saying the evening rosary in May; and at High School a powerful, insolent, and yet sensitive boy who got involved with numerous girls. For me the state of being an outcast and different became a source of distinction in these comrades, taking on the significance of freedom and self-determination. The outcast was the chosen one, the outstanding person – and there was nothing I longed for more than to be released from my social background.

As far back as I can remember, I lived out this state of release in my imagination. During my nursery days, I imagined every night that a fairy with long blonde hair and sparkling light blue eyes fetched me in her coach and took me to her kingdom. I was her favourite child. One day I told this fantasy to the boy next door as if it were a fact. He then asked me if he could also visit the fairy sometime. I answered that at dusk he should wait in front of my front door. He waited so long that his mother went in search of him – and then told the story to my mother. From that time onwards I was viewed as a liar and felt terribly ashamed. But that lie was my truth because it worked. What it brought about for me was that I had a mother who loved me without any reservations or conditions. The supposed lie was my mystery of love.

YOUNG HEROES

The final story from my childhood recalls myths, found in all cultures, of threatened, persecuted, and abandoned young heroes. They also had foster mothers and only discovered their destiny as outcasts and exiles. Oedipus was thus put in a chest and entrusted to the waters because his father Laius feared that his son would one day kill him. The story underlying that fear is little known. Laius stole the son of his host and friend Pelops so as to become his lover. Pelops then pronounced a curse against Laius, saying that his own son would do away with him. When Laius was tricked by his wife Jocasta – she made him drunk – into producing a son after all, he abandoned the boy, thus unwittingly creating the preconditions for Oedipus later killing the father he didn't know. A son often needs a great deal of distance from his father to be able to 'kill' him, which can entail breaking with the social conventions and norms the father embodies. That distance cannot be attained without the wound of love. Abandonment makes possible a new birth out of a new womb symbolised by the chest – or in the case of Moses, the future vehicle of the culture of the People of Israel, by a basket. Out of the fertile waters of the sea he enters upon a new land, upon a reality unencumbered by traditional ways.

Such heroes usually have something unexpected about themselves, which doesn't fit in with ideas about normal children. They sometimes suffer from some bodily deformation, as with Oedipus whose name means Club-Foot, or Pan as a miraculous child with goat's feet and horns, or Priapus whose entire body was nothing but a phallic symbol with its big tongue, mighty stomach, and huge phallus which grew instead of a tail. Parents do not want to identify with children different in that kind of way. Oedipus's abnormality is too reminiscent of distorted aspects of their own being.

Pan's great closeness to animality, instinct, and ecstasy calls into question the respectability and smothering of the body within everyday drudgery. Priapus's over-dimensional fertility and creativity upset psychological balance.

People thus distance themselves from this child so different to the others, withdrawing love from him for fear of being pulled into the vortex of tremendous vitality, which would disturb the apathy of a regulated existence. 'Normal' parents may do their duty with regard to this child, but that is too little. A child endowed with greater vitality needs greater love. Parents seem to tell a special child, usually wordlessly nowadays: 'You shouldn't be better off than we are'. That child is thus worse off. The parental setting is too constricted for its greater vitality. It needs more because it is more. If it gets less, it doesn't have enough. As elsewhere in human relations – think of Oscar Wilde and Alfred Douglas – the parental relationship to a special child involves the tyranny of the weaker over the stronger. Instead of growing towards the stronger, the weaker unconsciously attempts to cut down the other to his own size. If he finally succeeds, he despises the other as a reflection of his own weakness. Parents who have managed to break their children treat them like poor patients.

In the power struggle with their child, parents usually have things easier than a man fighting his wife, or vice versa, when both are adults. In fact, I know adults who are constantly overcome with rage and bitterness when they have once again, as in childhood, vainly endeavoured to storm the fortress occupied by their walled-in father or rejecting mother. They may long know that the love denied them when they were young is lost for ever, but they nevertheless still fight for it. Sometimes a client sits in front of me at the start of a session like an unloved child who wants to say: 'You take the first step. I always had to make the first move, and didn't achieve anything'.

If we look more closely at the manoeuvrings of now adult unloved children, we ascertain something astonishing. They do everything possible so as to be rejected. For instance, a forty year-old woman bombarded her eighty year old father with such reproaches and demands that in his weakness he had no alternative but to protect himself and forbid his daughter to visit him. Or a man of over fifty always spoke to his old mother, who had become cool and taciturn over the years, in such a whining voice that he got on her nerves. I am tempted to ask such a person: 'What do you really want?' – and sometimes I do. Unconsciously he wanted the fate that befalls 'heroes-to-be': to be rejected, or basically to fight his own way to freedom. And if we now take a closer look at the myths involving abandoned children, we understand why. Banishment brings fresh impulses for life as well as risks and danger.

Accounts of young heroes, who ultimately found a new home after withstanding many dangers, are always encouraging. Pan aroused fear in his mother. He was too boisterous and vital for her. Things would certainly not have gone well for him with such a mother. He was taken to Olympus by his father Hermes, and there he laughed and raised a commotion to the delight of all the immortals whose favourite he became. He was in the right surroundings and could let off steam. Greek gods – as embodiments of life-energy created by the human imagination – are not afraid of vitality. Pan, like all heroes, is a picture of vitality, a symbol of life-energy. Unlike Narcissus who fled the nymphs, Pan, who was also the son of a nymph, pursued them.

Perseus was able to laugh too. After being abandoned, he came upon some strange creatures, half man and half animal. He roared with laughter and rejoiced since he had, after all, found what he needed: contact with the instincts. That very laughter was interpreted by these creatures as a sign of his divine descent and as a vitality unconstrained by human conditions.

Laughter! Perseus laughed, Pan laughed, and Krishna also laughed – great outbursts of delight in life, surplus vitality freely cascading across the worlds, carefree convulsion of structures Wilhelm Reich viewed as nothing but frozen movement, and an expression of freedom and independence. Would Pan's mother have put up with her son's laughter? Probably not since she was afraid of him. How good that Pan is in a place where Homeric laughter is thought desirable.

Adult 'unloved children' should lose no time in following in the footsteps of Dionysos, who, according to one version of his story, didn't wait to be abandoned but instead ran off,

escaped from his pursuers into the sea, and found in a cave on
Crete the protection necessary for his development. By that I
mean that such people should no longer rely on being rejected
by their parents but should move towards independence on
their own initiative.

TAKING FROM ENEMIES

Greek myth provides 'unloved children' with another clue.
They should take all they need from people, even their
enemies. The young Heracles was abandoned by his mother
for fear of the jealous goddess Hera. When the goddess,
shrewdly guided by Athena, came to the place where the
child lay, she, once again led astray by Athena, took it
to her breast. Heracles was so powerful that he needed
ever more power, as is the case with vital children. He
sucked so impetuously at the Mother of All's breast that
she couldn't bear the pain, pulled the greedy child away,
and threw it to the ground. But Heracles had got what he
needed: divine, immortal vitality. Instead of storming old,
burnt-out fortresses, 'heroic children' would do better to gain
life where life is to be found. Amid the pain of being unloved,
they often forget that the reason for being unloved is their
greater vitality, and also their greater potential for love. In
order to allow the trauma of a lack of love during childhood
to 'grow over' (Jung), the fantasy of something missing
must be admitted. The lives of abandoned young heroes,
as depicted in myth, present such fantasies of something
lacking, necessary, and in need of fulfilment. For me the most
beautiful and richest mythological fantasy of compensation
for earlier love-wounds is the story of the joyous exile of the
divine youthful Krishna. His life was threatened by Rama, so
he spent his childhood among cow-herds – in other words,
among people close to the natural world and motherliness.
Krishna followed the other boys in clinging to cow's udders
and drinking his fill – just like Heracles at Hera's breast. For
years he did nothing except play and blow his flute.

If the psychological wound is not too deep, the unloved
child finds the freedom for its own life in play. In the case
of profoundly wounded people who could not play, it is
important during therapy to open up firstly small, and then

ever larger, areas for playing. I may take up something the client says, play with it, and then throw it back without any meaning or objective being involved. If he then notices that what seems pointless can be pleasurable, it also becomes meaningful to take up the problems that have led the client to therapy. The deadly idea of improvement has been broken through by means of playing. A wooden carving of the flute-playing Krishna hangs in my office to remind me that therapy is a game.

I wrote that solidarity with the world activates one's own life-energy. Krishna ate clay as if to assimilate the earth, and when he opened his mouth again the abundance of the whole of creation appeared there. When someone who has been rejected by established society and is unloved by 'model' human beings has survived the dangerous way of exile by water, he or she discovers union with the world and access to vitality.

When playing with other boys, Krishna imitated the buzzing of bees and the cuckoo's call, mimicked passing birds, and leapt like an ape from branch to branch. As he hopped in the water like a frog and saw his reflection, he laughed.[1] By observing himself, he also confirms the joyous freedom of his destiny, which is what the unloved and deprived most need. He changes the perspective. From being dependent on his parents he becomes someone open to the world, to birds, bees, frogs, apes, and to instinctive relationship and vitality.

How different, however, is our world from Krishna's idyll of childhood! And yet the attitude to our polluted and contaminated world must be the same: play, dedication, and love – so as to strengthen the 'will to health' in both our organism and the sick environment. We won't know what healing action to take if we lack intensive fantasies about the beauty and power of life.

THE ATTRACTION OF PINOCHIO

The myth of the heroic child pursues the opposite path to didactic picaresque novels. The former releases a human being to freedom and self-determination, whilst the latter have as their objective constraint of the untamed child, the wild 'Krishna', within the norms of bourgeois society, bringing about 'voluntary' conformity through various tricks and appeals to love of parents. Pinocchio is a typical example of that. He moves from freedom to compliance rather than developing, like the heroic child, from conformism to liberty. Yet why do we find Pinocchio so sympathetic? Because of his success in conforming? Once that is achieved, the story comes to an end. Pinocchio is no longer interesting, lacks individual and special characteristics, lacks joy and exuberance. Of course, human development also includes adaptation to norms and customs. If that doesn't happen, there occur symptoms of abandonment similar to those found in someone who conforms excessively and loves himself too little. Excessive conformism continues, however, to be a much more widespread problem than avoidance of commitments and responsibility. The story of most of the unloved is one of over-adaptation. Such people need to develop a new attitude to outcasts, pariahs, and un-touchables.

The unconscious yearnings of a conformist making up for lack of love are directed towards establishing inner contact with what is untouched and rejected, thereby liberating a Krishna bubbling over with joy in the world and life. What does that mean? The pariah may be rejected but he is also free of the obligations of those who cast him out. He has access to a world closed to the well-regulated and the insured, a world of unchannelled life-energy and shadowy, ambivalent fantasies. Passion for the pariah urges every unloved person towards freedom. Could it not be that the outsider himself played a part in conditioning his parents so as to become a pariah – in other words, someone who is not particularly loved by the well-regulated, and thanks to that fact, enjoys more personal liberty? Be that as it may, he has greater talent for freedom than other people, greater talent and also a greater urge.

No other film has ever moved me so much as François Truffaut's *Les quattre cent coups*. I saw it at Saint-Maurice where I was attending the French-speaking High School. The film tells the story of a boy who is stuck in a reformatory. He dreams of seeing the sea, breaks out, and finally does get to the sea. Truffaut was telling his own story there. Only someone rejected and unloved could feel this yearning for the sea so strongly. Truffaut succeeded in transforming the pariah that suffering' speak words that Jesus applies to himself: 'I am a

SIX

Renunciation of Belated Parental Love

Parental love cannot be compelled. If it was absent, the daughter or son sometimes strives, their life long, to gain such love – not just from their actual parents, who may perhaps long be dead, but also from anyone of importance in their lives. He (or she) thus remains a dependent child, and development is blocked. The wound of the unloved cannot heal. Here I take up and extend this idea from the previous chapter. Only renunciation of parental love that comes too late breaks this spell.

The word 'renunciation' can result in the wrong assumption that this necessary process can be implemented just by an act of will. That is not the case. All those who are unloved know that mere declarations of intent are of no use in this sphere, and that therapy consisting only of good advice merely discourages people even more. An intellectual psychology which only appeals to common sense does not achieve anything here. The renunciation I am talking about derives from insight into previously unconscious interrelationships. Those are the subject of what follows.

First I will consider the simpler case of the self-willed child which goes its own way, increasingly deviating from the parents. Then I'll turn to the more difficult case of the weak adult 'child', in need of loving care, that was not taken seriously by its parents, which is an expression of lack of love. Finally, I explain why no one finds it easy to renounce childish expectations, even though human maturation depends on that. Renunciation of parental love is demanded of everyone. Let me say once again that I use the word 'unloved' for all degrees of insufficiency in parental love. This general usage is psychologically justified since, despite all the differences involved, such a lack of parental love always produces the same outcome in a child: many gradations and nuances in lack of self-love and primal confidence. I am more concerned with common aspects than with the differences, even though I will also stress those. The most important reason for that lies even deeper. Healing of the psychological wound ultimately takes place through gaining access to a profound level where all human beings are the same. The misfortune of a lack of parental love cannot be eliminated, but can be instead viewed in connection with the experience of an existential lack entailed in being a human being. By that I mean the absence of security in this world. Healing goes no further than that. Attention will be devoted at a later stage to the link between the lack resulting from particular circumstances and the sense of something missing which is part of the human condition. This initial mention is intended to establish why I utilise the word 'unloved' in undifferentiated fashion for all forms of absence of love. They derive from something existential. Viewed in those terms, the word 'unloved' refers to an existential feeling rather than just a deficiency based on demonstrable facts.

Literature is full of examples of ostracism of non-conformists by parents and society. Such a conflict has always been one of the most frequent motives impelling an author to take up his pen. In his novel *America* Franz Kafka describes how Karl Rossmann from Prague is rejected by his parents because of a relationship with a servant girl. *Anna Karenina* in Tolstoy's novel and Melanie in Fontane's *L'adultera* are attacked as adulteresses. The former kills herself and the latter learns responsibility and freedom. Many parents today still behave towards their rebellious children as bourgeois society once reacted towards adultery.

Literature also deals with the subject of the stronger from whom the weaker resentfully withhold love. In Franz Werfel's story *Der Abiturient[e]ntag*, the brooding young Franz Adler, emanating the authority of 'unwavering truthfulness', is tormented, humiliated, and finally broken by the narrator, Sebastian. People who are different from others and thus more vulnerable are often also excluded from love and destroyed within their families. Their ultimate downfall then serves as confirmation that the withholding of love was justified from the start.

WHY PEOPLE TURN TO THERAPY

Such people often start therapy. They feel that something is crooked within themselves, and must be straightened out so as to grow. They want to awaken out of the social hypnosis of their supposed inferiority and discover their real value. For that they have to comprehend the play of powers where they were the victim. They were oppressed because they were dangerous. They were dangerous because they were superior. Awareness of their real superiority constitutes the first step on their way towards self-esteem and self-love. By supporting this process I certainly do not further fantasies of omnipotence, but rather awareness of facts which were hitherto obscured in favour of other people's claims to power. Establishment of the real superiority of the person concerned is dependent on correct analysis of the family situation. Such a person will find encouragement in the following declaration by Sloterdijk even if he isn't amoral: 'Frankly, the amoral have my unlimited sympathy since they make space . . . for life, whereas virtuous citizens with their hundred compulsive ideas already give you a taste of what they will do to others.'[1]

A younger woman, who was one of those unloved out of envy, told the following dream. She was on a street in Zürich together with her mother, but somehow the two of them didn't make any progress. Then she realised that she was supposed to show her mother the way to the 'Freudenberg' ('Hill of Joy'), a Zürich park where there is a school. The mother harrassed and reproached her daughter because she didn't really know the way. Such criticism really confused the dreamer. The two of them got lost. The dreamer finally gave up looking for the 'Freudenberg' and couldn't even find her car again. She told her mother she absolutely had to go and meet the man who had already been waiting an hour for her. The mother reacted by intensifying her reproaches, calling her an ungrateful daughter and a useless creature. The two carried on walking, but the daughter knew that she was getting ever further away from where the friend was waiting for her. She awoke with a feeling of destruction.

While the woman told her dream, I didn't merely pay attention to its contents. I also observed the energy pattern which became apparent. By that I mean the specific succession of diverse movements of life-energy characteristic of a certain person. Several dreams with different subject matter can demonstrate the same energy pattern. That also occurs in an individual's other expressions, not just in dreams. The same individual has several energy patterns whose activation depends on the situation. The dream's energy pattern can be schematically presented as follows.

1. Initially movement is laborious and slow (no real progress is made).
2. Two impulses appear within this movement: one urging forwards (the mother hounding her daughter), and the other holding back (the daughter who doesn't find the way her mother wants to take).
3. The inhibiting impulse becomes stronger and leads to confused movements (the two get lost).
4. An attempt at a progression of energy fails (the dreamer doesn't find the car with which she'd like to drive to her friend).
5. Finally there occurs a regression of energy (she gets even further away from where the man lives). (I have followed C.G. Jung in my use of the terms progression and regression.)

In talking about the dream, I try to avoid losing awareness of the energy pattern so as not to further increase confusion. Energy patterns constitute an important guide towards the interpretation of dreams. They demonstrate what is ultimately at issue. Awareness of the energy pattern prevents the analytical discussion going astray in dream symbolism so that you no longer see the wood for the trees. During the course of our conversation the dreamer said: 'Yes, I always do that. To begin with I don't completely know what I really want. One argument is in favour of something, another against. I do what others want of me. Then resistance develops. That leads to states of confusion which can last for days. I have less and less energy, and try in vain to get things moving again. Then my guilt feelings increase, I give in, and do what others expect, or what my guilt feelings say. And yet I constantly make mistakes there. Nothing goes right any longer. Everything that seems important and valuable to me has vanished. I miss out on what is most important of all'. This woman told me about several scenes in her everyday existence where this energy pattern received expression. That always happened when she wanted to undertake something that really moved her.

MAKING CONNECTIONS

Psycho-energetic analysis – in this case analysis of an energy pattern conducted at the same time as analysis of content – has the advantage that it reveals the connection between the most diverse events. It is comparable with structural analysis of literary texts. This may seem somewhat sober to the reader, but my experience is that people are very struck when the inhibiting energy pattern is laid bare. They often react with such sentences as: 'At long last I've understood!' or 'That's what counts!' Consciousness of an energy pattern amidst critical situations offers inner feedback, which sometimes leads to immediate changes of behaviour. There is a mounting feeling of having at last grasped the nature of the constricting life-plan. What previously seemed to be insolubly complicated falls into place.

Body analysis – analysis of the dynamics of bodily movements – is also a part of this process. During the telling of her 'typical stories', the woman's body revealed the phases of her energy pattern. To begin with, she made unspecific but still co-ordinated movements; then she succumbed to a 'little storm' of checked, nervous, unco-ordinated movements; became ever more rigid and stiff; and finally collapsed. I knew this pattern of movement from many situations when she told me about a problem.

Energy patterns are dynamic, not static. They are characteristic sequences of movement. What is at issue here is developing a sense of energy at work: compulsive, inhibited, confusedly petering away, or flowing back again. Body analysis is an indispensable aspect of comprehending an energy pattern. All the same, it should be employed with restraint and great sensitivity or else it is more likely to inhibit the client.

Just a few remarks now on the dream and its dreamer. This was a sympathetic woman, successful in her career and a much stronger personality than her mother. She had studied against her mother's will. At the age of thirty she got to know a man in whose company she for the first time felt: 'I want this partnership. It makes me happy, and takes me further'. When this daughter was three, her mother had got divorced. Since that time the daughter had felt pursued by her mother's reproaches and envy. The mother often bewailed her difficult situation as a divorced woman, and made use of her daughter whenever she could. She also took over the daughter's first boy-friend. Time and again she stressed how much she had given the daughter, but took unjustifiably much from her. When my client was together with her current friend, she was often afflicted by guilt feelings about her mother.

In her dreams she once again sought her mother's joy ('Freudenberg') rather than her own. But she cannot know her mother's way to joy because they are two different people. In addition she feels resistance to the mother's laying claim to seeking the way in her place and taking over responsibility for her. Hence the many ifs and buts. Such resistance leads her to feel guilty (the mother's reproaches in the dream). Guilt feelings diminish her initiative, only allowing one thing to develop: the same resistance that led to the initial guilt feelings. Now she is completely blocked. The thought of her friend arises within as a memory of personal joy, but merely so as to make clear to her that the more she gets involved with the mother the more she cuts herself off from love of this man and of her own existence.

Contemplation of her dream enabled the woman to understand that every time she made these indefinite, nervous, and checked movements at the start of some activity or enterprise, she really didn't want to do what she was involved in and was adapting to someone else as in the dream. The mother's 'Hill of Joy' was not hers. She became more aware of starting points where she was denying herself. She gradually became able to avoid getting involved in enterprises to which formerly she had only agreed so as to please others. From that time onwards she recognised her involuntary, nervous movements as a signal: 'You're starting to conform again. Do you really want that?' The new awareness attained through body analysis thus made a decision possible for her even in situations where compulsiveness had hitherto prevailed. Her self-confidence grew at the same time. She began to realise that she was not subordinate to her mother, and didn't therefore need to accord the mother power over her life. Renunciation of belated mother love was under way.

She also recognised the danger of pity, which makes such renunciation more difficult. Won't the mother become more deprived if she, the daughter, no longer woos her? Can the mother continue to exist at all if the daughter keeps her distance? Shouldn't she (the daughter) leave the mother her pleasure in saying 'No'? The danger involved in pity was the most difficult for the daughter to surmount? But she had to liberate herself there so as to be able to really love her friend and herself. Nietzsche's warning with regard to love of neighbour also applied to her: 'Woe to all lovers whose aspiration is limited to pity'.[2]

COMPLICITY

Anyone who has profound insight into such entanglements with parents is no longer tempted to believe they are the sole cause of his problems. He senses that *cause and effect* are merely 'conventional fictions serving labelling and communication rather than explanation'.[3] Complicity exists in all relationships, even between children and parents. I view complicity as involving participation rather than shared responsibility. Someone who accepts that insight feels impelled towards activity and individual responsibility within the here and now. The 'occurrence' becomes an 'experience', and rejection a striking out into freedom. Experiencing oneself as a doer rather than a sufferer is a sign of vitality. I do not of course want to trivialise the tragedy of innumerable childhood wounds, but rather to motivate people to take action in the present.

Don't there exist people who are too weak to be able to do without the parental love and care a child needs? Even the weakest of the unloved possesses a spark of the strong 'hero-to-be', a slight possibility of transforming other people's early 'No' into a 'Yes' towards himself. The sense of deficiency is an indication of an unutilised potential for personal activity. Such a spark can be recognised – albeit as the outcome of patient empathy – even in many psychotics, as is stressed by R.D. Laing, the British psychiatrist.

At the start of his analysis, a man of about forty dreamed of his father under whose shadow he had spent his entire life. He was intelligent, capable in his job, yet fearful and sickly. His dead father appeared to him in a dream, and reproachfully said how sad he was that his son still bowed and scraped. When talking to me the dreamer remarked: 'How can I stop being subservient when he still influences me so much?' The father's dual message to his son: 'Don't bow and scrape any longer' and 'Stay overshadowed by me' demonstrates why the son thought he was too weak a man to do without 'parental love' – that is, the love of people whom he used as substitute parents.

His manliness remains trapped between his father's contradictory messages: 'Be a man' and 'I'm the only man'. What a great deal of energy was expended on submitting until he really was bowed down! Melting this frozen energy so that it starts to flow is only possible if the son can unmask the father's second message – I'm the only man. Your place is to be overshadowed by me' – as a lie. It is the unloved person who feels too weak that most urgently needs to renounce parental love. Too much energy is bound up in his desperate yearning: does the weak person he believes himself to be really exist? Wasn't a great deal of strength needed in order to make himself so weak? Hasn't his strength concealed itself behind weakness? Doesn't he play along in his father's game? Doesn't his view of cause and effect – that is, of the mighty father who deprives the son of power – conceal a trick so as to keep his strength in reserve? It is time for him to enter into the light!

This man had a phobia about the sun. He shunned sunlight, associating it with sun-burn, sun-stroke, skin cancer, damage to the eyes, and also an overwhelming fear of being seen. If he were surprised by the sun, the itching from which he almost always suffered became worse. He wasn't free and sought security in the darkness and in the shadow of other people – unlike Diogenes, who asked Alexander the Great to stand out of his light.

This client once observed to me that he associated the sun with the unbearable suffering of Roman slaves. That was the decisive clue. Who was the invisible slave owner? None other than his father, the inner image of his father who forbade him to view life as anything but drudgery beneath the pitiless light and merciless gaze of the slave driver. He had never felt a warming sun in his father's regard. 'Perhaps he did after all love me', the man once said, 'but I never felt it'.

Sunlight gradually took on a new quality for him. Blinking cautiously, he ventured, briefly and furtively, into the open air, beginning to guess that light could really also signify growth, seeing oneself as well as being seen, and oneself shedding rather than being deprived by others. The itching slowly diminished. The wish to slip out of his skin and slave away for others became increasingly infrequent. His hump 'melted' – in other words, he straightened up and, head on high, began to look around. This was a slow process of feeling his way forwards with many setbacks. It is particularly important for such deeply wounded people to know that the termination of analysis does not mean the end of all symptoms and taking normality for granted. What is involved is a sense of direction, and an instinct for light as a guiding principle.

Towards the end of our prolonged shared work he brought me Plato's metaphor of the cave, which he had typed out. 'That was my story' he said. 'If someone were actually to leave the cave, he would be blinded by the sun and see nothing', he quoted, and continued: 'I lived for long with nothing but shadows which objects threw on the wall – out of fear that reality was pitiless like my father'. When we concluded our work, he stood beneath the entrance to the cave on the threshold between a shadowy existence and openness. He retained the possibility of occasionally retreating into the protective darkness if he once again encountered the slave driver's gaze. A sense of direction and an instinct for light as a guiding principle are not the only preconditions for termination of analysis. These also include knowledge of the strategies required for being able to trick old ghosts. It was desirable for my client to do the same as Zarathustra at the conclusion of

Nietzsche's work: '. . . left his cave, glowing and strong, like a morning sun emerging from behind dark mountains'.[4] Was Zarathustra right to leave the cave completely?

HEALING THE WOUND

It is not just people who were wounded at an early age that must renounce parental love. This is the outcome of everyone's urge towards development and autonomy. That must be briefly mentioned here. It is necessary, wrote Jung in his *Symbols of Transformation*, that 'All the libido tied up in family bonds be withdrawn from the narrower circle into the larger one. . . .'[5] The *victim* of parental love is dedication to life. Many people feel they are unloved because they do not succeed in loving themselves. If they were to stop scratching away at the wound of being unloved, it could heal more quickly. But as long as someone doesn't open his hands to others, he remains curled up like an embryo, Luther's unredeemed man (*'homo in se incorvatus'*). Jung adds that 'The sacrifice of the libido that strives back to the past necessarily results in the creation of the world'[6], in creation of one's own life within the relationship to the world. The maternal cave itself presses the hesitant foetus into the light. Isn't this lack of love a greater love? Don't we like moaning about things that are necessary for us?

In the same connection Jung explains the universally disseminated incest taboo. This is intended to prevent us from returning to what went before rather than being reborn, and from eroticising (through distorted adaptation to our parents) what has to discharge us into the world instead of becoming free for that world. 'It cannot have been the incest taboo that forced mankind out of the original psychic state of non-differentiation. On the contrary, it was the evolutionary instinct peculiar to man, which . . . forced upon him countless taboos, among them the incest taboo'.[7] The developmental instinct brings about renunciation of belated parental love whose expectation paralyses rather than nourishes an adult.

SEVEN

The Open Wound
of Depression

Inability to accept the necessity of renunciation of parental love can lead to depression. Not that every depressive adult demands unconditional love of his or her parents by birth. But since that demand has never been met, it is transferred to the person to whom he or she relates most closely, usually one's companion through life. If the person concerned does not then receive the unquestioning love which only a small child needs and can experience, he perhaps becomes depressive. In any case he finds such love lacking since even the partner's most devoted love is not enough for someone who expects parental adoration. The most manifest devotion and love is too little. All demonstrations of solidarity, faithfulness, reliability and dedication are unconsciously measured against unfulfilled demands made of the father or mother – and faulted. He then mistakenly feels he has lost the other, even when the partner is very close.

I don't know a single depressive whose sufferings do not originate in early experiences of withheld or misdirected love, leading to inability to renounce what has been denied. Coming to terms with childhood is therefore an important, if not the only, method whereby the depressive find their way out into the world. There is no other biographical explanation for the fact that some people react to the loss of a loved one with grief and others with depression. In *Mourning and Melancholia* Freud explains the difference between the two without investigating the causes of grief in the one case and depression in the other. The biographical reason is sufficiency or insufficiency of love during childhood. Depression can only be avoided if parental love during childhood was sufficient to outweigh severe adult loss and the profound pain resulting from present separation. What we call predisposition is often early shaping whereby the personal character concerned also of course plays a more or less important part. From the first moment onwards, human existence is the outcome of interactions between internal and external influences. We are creatures of relationship.

In 1917 Freud still used the word 'melancholia' for what we call 'depression'. Today we make a distinction between the two states. Melancholia is an existential state that overcomes someone when he encounters the transience of all things, 'weeping tears over things' ('sunt lacrimae rerum' as Vergil writes. Depression, on the other hand, entails just what Freud in 1917 characterised as melancholia. To that we now turn our attention.

Freud writes: 'Melancholia (that is, depression) is psychologically characterised by a profoundly pain-stricken mood, suspension of interest in the outer world, loss of capacity for love, obstruction of any activity, and belittling of the feeling of selfhood, which receives expression in self-reproach and self-abuse, and intensifies to the point of delusory expectation of punishment'.[1]

COMING TO TERMS WITH LOSS

The process of mourning liberates life-energy from the link with the loved person now lost. It attempts to come to terms with the reality of the loss. 'Where loss was suffered, mourning is the natural consequence' (A. and M. Mitscherlich). That, however, is precisely what does not occur in depression. A depressive identifies himself with the person now lost, remaining fused with him or her. He 'does not consciously grasp what he has lost, even if he knows who he has lost'.[2] He doesn't, for instance, know that with this partner he has lost a feeling for himself because in fusing with the person now vanished he denied himself.

How do the bitter self-reproaches, the guilt feelings, and the tendency towards self-punishment which can lead to suicide, come about? The depressive, writes Freud, 'takes revenge on the original objects by the roundabout way of self-punishment'. That also explains 'the importunate talkativeness, finding satisfaction in unmasking oneself'. Unmasking oneself thus signifies exposure of the other, and aggression against oneself hostility towards the other. Freud also explains 'the mystery of an inclination towards suicide' in this way.[3]

Freud mentions another point contributing towards the understanding of depression. I believe this is a central issue, and would like to intensify and extend it in psycho-energetic terms. He writes: 'In mourning the world has become poor; in melancholia (that is, depression) it is the ego itself'.[4] The person who grieves is realistic in facing up to the loss suffered. His personality can become richer and more mature even if the world has become poorer. A depressive, on the other hand, loses himself along with the person lost. 'The melancholia complex behaves like an open wound, attracting occupying energies from all sides and emptying the ego to the point of impoverishment'.[5] The open wound of depression attracts what is alien and rejects what is one's own.

The depressive is fused with the lost 'love object' so he becomes identical with its loss, forfeiting his own ability to love. His relationship has become a void, so he feels himself to be nothing. He makes the other's turning away, whether real or imagined, into an estrangement from himself. The emptiness left behind by the lost relationship becomes a vacuum within himself. He does what he feels the lost 'love object' did to him: he leaves himself, annuls his own existence, and through his life confirms the fact that the other has left him.

Unlike Freud, I am not of the opinion that self-reproaches and the depressive's inclination towards suicide exclusively signify a reversal of aggression, which is really directed towards the lost 'love object'. I see the most important reason for the self-destructive impulse as lying deeper. Fusion with the other is so total that it also includes the other's act of abandonment. That is therefore the same as turning away from oneself. The unconscious logic of depression is the final act in a love involving total fusion: 'How right you were to leave me! I am also leaving myself, thereby remaining united with you. Love cannot go further than that. I will keep you for ever by losing myself. The further away you go, the closer I am, since I go with you, away from myself'. So the

most important cause of depression is misdirected love. Love moves everything – both forwards and backwards.
Depression doesn't only occur as the result of an actual loss. It's often independent of such loss. Even if not sparked off by the actual loss of someone close, depression always derives from resurrection of a previous 'love object' from whom one is insufficiently separated. In all instances there prevails the unconscious logic that a turning away from oneself signifies faithfulness to the lost other.

DEPRESSIVE SELF-LOVE

Let us now consider the dynamics of depressive self-loss as viewed in psycho-energetics. Instead of being attracted by the external world and confronted by one's own existence, thereby releasing energy, a depressive allows himself to be coerced from outside, thus feeling oppressed and forced down, which is after all the original meaning of depressed. He thus restricts energy, only feeling a demand and no individual initiative, only guilt feelings and no responsibility. He exerts counter-pressure against the pressure supposedly coming from outside, preventing himself from moving or falling. If he falls, that is involuntary.

I will now investigate the *energy pattern* – the pattern of psychological movement – involved in four dreams experienced by people with more or less severe depressions. A slightly depressive woman dreamt she was wearing a bathing costume, standing on a lake-side diving board, but didn't dare jump in. Instead of actively yielding to the force of gravity, the dreamer resists. Nevertheless she wants to jump and is attracted downwards. Experiencing and tolerating that wish is a remarkable step forwards. It remains, however, nothing but a wish. She is thinking too soon. It would be soon enough to think about what has been done after actually jumping. Anyone who thinks too soon thinks too little. As a result the woman distances herself from the original wish. Energy flows out of the wish into the thinking which creates distance. She has thus spent her life up to now on the diving board, attracted by the natural flow of things but fearful of the unknown. She doesn't allow herself to be attracted. She is always just about to do something, just going to jump. She is weighed down by an external heaviness because she doesn't yield to her own gravity.

A clear-cut energy pattern receives expression in this brief dream. Anyone who devotes attention to their energy patterns will constantly encounter them. The dawning of consciousness that thus occurs is not an interpretation, but merely a reflection of what I am doing. That is repeatedly described in the teachings of the Buddha in such terms as: 'A walking monk recognises "I am walking"; a standing monk sees "I am standing"; a sitting monk knows "I am sitting"' and so on. We direct the reflecting consciousness towards steps within the process of an energy pattern. Whatever needs changing will gradually change of its own accord just because we do not want to change it deliberately.

What energy pattern constitutes the dynamic structure within the dream of the woman who doesn't jump into the water, regardless of the differing situations which bring it to life? The dreamer was able to answer as follows:

1. Life attracts me.
2. I want to risk something.
3. I immediately think about that.
4. I distance myself from my wish.
5. My resistance contains more energy than my wish.
6. I wait and see.

Every phase within a psychological energy pattern must be made conscious – without reflection – through just perceiving the movements of energy. Complete, undivided attention is very important, leaving no energy for self-reproaches. If they should nevertheless develop, we immediately say: 'I'm reproaching myself'. This exercise, which is taught in Zen, is astonishingly effective over the long-term, and particularly during critical periods. It promotes the flow of consciousness and intensifies prolonged attentiveness. I know a woman whose periodic attacks of anxiety vanished without any psychotherapy being necessary – thanks solely to this exercise.

Another energy pattern characteristic of the depressed is revealed in the following dream by a thirty five year-old man. 'I am sitting at the steering wheel of our family car, which is climbing up a steep incline. My wife and three children

are in the car with me. I stop in the middle of this ascent.
Now the brakes don't function any longer. The car almost
rolls backwards into the valley'.

Despite everything, the brakes do stop the car plunging
downwards. That was not always the case. The dreamer
had previously regularly succumbed to depressive losses of
energy and states of dependence on familiar surroundings.
Compared with that he had already mobilised more energy,
but not enough to get up the steep incline. Unlike the previous dreamer, this man had no difficulty in allowing himself
to fall from time to time, enjoying life in particular situations.
He nonetheless has difficulty in coping with everyday burdens, which frequently rob him of zest. I limit myself here
to description of the energy-pattern in his dream. The man
might express that as follows:

1. Things are improving, and there's energy.
2. A burden weighs me down (in this case his family,
   but he always found something).
3. I don't get any further and come to a stop.
4. I lose energy.
5. I can prevent myself from falling back.

Those five steps occurred time and again within different
situations in the dreamer's current existence. The energy
bound up in stopping on a steep incline – that is, in struggling
against depression – is lost *for* life. If he becomes aware of his
energy pattern's five phases within a situation itself rather
than in retrospect, he experiences himself as someone taking
action. Something will then be slowly transformed in the
final step where a change for the better is already becoming
apparent. The man used to fall into a hole at the conclusion of
a neurotic cycle. In future he will probably no longer stop on a
slope but rather on the level so as to rest before surmounting
difficult life-situations in one sweep.

ESCAPING FRUSTRATIONS

The unloved lack a sense of critical cycles in their own
lives because they reject everything imperfect in themselves.
Recognising one's own obstructing energy patterns sharpens

that sense. When paying attention to these patterns such people are completely focused without being sucked into the slipstream of the frustrations suffered in childhood. They gain detachment from those frustrations by completely devoting themselves to today's energy patterns. They thereby gain strength to deal more actively with burdensome situations. Paying attention to their own energy patterns makes self-acceptance tangible.

I conclude my thoughts on the open wound of depression with two dreams by a forty year old woman. The interaction between analysis of subject matter and energy patterns will be demonstrated here. The first dream intensified the depression already afflicting the woman. 'I'm together with my husband. He tells me that a colleague at work has drawn his attention to my unbecoming appearance. I am the worst looking woman of all. And Mrs X the most beautiful. He (the dreamer's husband) then asked another colleague, who was also of the opinion that I wasn't beautiful. So I asked my husband: "What do you think about that?" He was evasive: "It's all right by me". I press him further so that he should at long last provide relief and say: "You're beautiful" – but he doesn't. He finally asks me whether we should do something together, but I'm too tired and tell him so'.

This dream is particularly revealing because the dreamer is in fact an exceptionally beautiful woman, and her husband often praises her for that with total conviction. In her original family things were, however, completely different. The mother constantly criticised her four children's appearance, and these youngsters continued this malicious game among themselves. Within this family exchange at least one part of every child's body 'was' ridiculous and ugly. One had a long neck and a small head, another had fat ankles, a third stank and was disgusting in general, and she, the fourth, had hips which were too broad. A competition developed between the four of them. Each compared himself or herself with the others, observing who got the largest piece of meat and taking revenge on the person who seemed to be favoured. The compulsion towards comparison in a loveless competition also receives expression in the dream. 'Mirror, mirror, on the wall, who is fairest of them all?' asks the wicked queen in *Snow White*, who cannot love because she herself feels unloved. A look into the mirror, craving recognition, is intended to replace the loving regard of someone close. That doesn't work, however. So she looks into the mirror time and again, always finding someone more beautiful, which she had always 'known'. She then wants to eliminate, to devalue, that other person so as to rid herself of the torment of her own inferiority. She becomes a wicked mother out of rage against her competitor. The enviable beauty in turn succumbs to an inferiority complex. The fatal interconnection persists. That is how family destinies are established.

When the mirror signifies a mother substitute, we are terribly dependent on other people's judgement. We also remain stuck in externalities, and seek to please. An agreeable judgement can lead us to forget our emptiness for a short time, but doubt soon makes its presence felt again. Did he really mean that seriously? Wasn't he flattering me? Or: what does one person's judgement amount to? What do other people think about me? Do I please them? The dreamer was thus dependent on her mother as a child? She craved for the mother to say, loud and clear, what she hoped of her husband in the dream: 'I like you, and you please me just as you are'. But the mother was always evasive: 'Yes, you did that well', and 'Today you please me better than yesterday. But try to plait your hair more attractively tomorrow'. This woman's childhood was spent trying in vain to gain acceptance of her person as a whole. She never felt that her mother loved her without ifs and buts. In fact her mother didn't love her. Love relates to the whole of a human being, not to individual aspects of appearance and character, or individual actions. She thus put herself under pressure to do well: 'I must change that, no this, no that, or perhaps something completely different?' And her mother made her believe that whatever she was changing at that moment wasn't the crucial thing. If the daughter strove today to deal with yesterday's criticism, something else came under attack. That showed her that the mother didn't even pay any attention to her efforts to please but instead wiped them out by blaming her for something else.

In her marriage the forty year-old gradually lost the inner relationship to her husband, believed his affection was a lie and illusion, and identified with his supposed rejection: 'Yes, you're right. I also avoid myself. I completely

merge with your "No" as I used to do with my mother's
"No". She overwhelmed herself with bitter reproaches and
contemplated suicide. From time to time she allowed herself
to be intellectually convinced that her husband loved her, but
she didn't feel that. Entangled in destructive dependence,
she was often tired and incapacitated. The only part of her
dream which accorded with everyday reality was the last. Her
husband really had asked her the previous evening whether
she would like to do something together with him, but she
was too tired for that. The dream uncovered the background
to her weariness.

There is a familiar saying that love makes beautiful. That's
true. It's also true that we think beautiful someone we love.
Augustine characterised beauty as the splendour of truth.
Splendour is radiance, resplendence, life-energy, love. And
truth is every word, every glance, every gesture that exerts an
undistorted influence on us. So beauty as the glory of truth
is an outcome of love – and love is compelling. Someone
who loves truly disseminates such splendour that it would
be eccentric to call in question – on aesthetic grounds –
the beauty that is openly revealed. 'Beauties' from sales
catalogues are lonely, lacking splendour and truth. The
dreamer's longing for beauty entails her longing for love.

The dreamer's subjugation to external authority is particularly apparent in this dream. She feels no energy, which
should vitally emerge out of herself. She therefore believes
herself dependent on an external source of energy. But even
when life from outside penetrates her, she merely experiences that as demands and pressures, feeling overtaxed and
depressed.

FAMILY ENERGY PATTERNS

During analysis she and I paid attention to even the least
movements of energy from within herself – in other words,
to what derived from her rather than from somewhere else
– and we ascertained the energy pattern determined by
her family. 'You have everything, and I've got nothing' or
'You've got all the energy, and I none'. Then she brought the
following dream. 'I return home after a long war. Everything
is devastated: our house, the other houses, all the streets –

a huge, desolate landscape. In the midst of this devastation stands a large tree. This has four mighty roots between which the trunk rises on high. Afterwards I see the tree's four roots geometrically from above as four circles which group themselves around a central circle of the same size'.

The dreamer really cannot build life as an adult on her childhood. The necessary process of destruction has been achieved, and the hollow facades lie broken on the ground. Now that she has finished with her childhood, she becomes aware of the tree, the tree of life. As long as she was still dependent on what now lies in ruins, the world in which she grew up, she didn't yet know about this tree. She didn't sense her potential for growth. Now the tree stands there in all its beauty, an image of dynamic wholeness. In my office there hangs a Nepalese mandala depicting the ordering of the five circles. The dreamer had assimilated this, and brought about its resurrection in her dream as the order of growth within her life: a framework for the regaining of health rather than a pattern of illness.

People who experienced early devastation cannot build on the world of their childhood and adolescence. They need clear-cut, inner images of their growth, images of the objectives of vitality. The dreamer's tree of life grows out of the ruins of her old world. It needs a new world where it can flourish. The woman started to turn her gaze to the world around. Did that really consist only of dependences bombed to smithereens? In opening her eyes she gained strength. She began to become aware of people who loved her. In the process she noticed that she loved too.

The purpose of a depression entails gaining freedom from old, inhibiting life-plans. We can become depressive when the impulse towards transformation starts to be apparent and at the same time former burdens incapacitate. Depressions aim at new creation. Isn't it the case that creative people are particularly afflicted by depressive phases in their lives, times when life-energy is blocked and they sense themselves lacking in initiative, tormented, and feeling full of weary restlessness and guilt? And then suddenly, initially almost unnoticed, the inner current forces its way into life again with new words, images, and gestures. Creative power does not signify eagerness to work, but rather creation which makes work necessary. Isn't everyone creative in his or her growth? Isn't he or she many times condemned to death, to destruction of dependences which yesterday seemed likely to last for sweet eternity? Man drives himself out of paradises which have ceased to exist.

EIGHT

Identity in Longing

A re human beings divided into the loved and the unloved: those who received sufficient love during childhood and those who didn't? The question alone produces a shaking of the head in disbelief. But I want to persist. Is it merely the fact of the sliding scale involved in the best and worst possible amounts of love received during childhood that makes my initial question so absurd? Are the problems approached in this book, involving the feeling of being unloved, only of interest to people who really were and are little loved? Couldn't it be that this is more than just a personal problem, that it is a problem affecting human existence as such, beyond all biographical data, and that everyone suffers in an existential sense from the wound of being unloved? I cannot conclude this second part of the book, entitled 'Understanding', without having awoken appreciation of this issue. In the fifteenth chapter I shall return to the same question from a different perspective.

Longing is a strange feeling: an urgent 'joy-sorrow feeling'. The heart beats happily and sadly at the same time. Eroticism is involved too. We situate love and longing in the same part of the body – in the middle of the chest at the level of the heart where people suffering from such feelings press their hands. Some epochs mention this yearning more than others (for instance Romanticism more than Realism). Some nations are experts in longing. In Brazil no word is spoken with such feeling as 'saudade' – not even the word 'love'. Isn't it the excitement of yearning, that agitating amalgam of quenching a thirst and painful lack, that makes love so delightful? Isn't the exhilaration of longing so brilliant just because it is overshadowed? Cannot unutterable longing seize hold of us even amid the greatest happiness?

Love involves the tension of insistent feelings between two people. Even when lovers rest, a subtle tension quivers between them. At the start of an encounter between lovers, this tension is apparent in pushing and shoving, tugging and pulling. In love yearning reaches out for what doesn't yet exist. At the same time, love points backwards to what is no longer, in retrospective longing. A single moment of love extends into the remotest past and future. The more attentive we are, the further its horizons extend. Moments of love are thus always moments of yearning, and our wings are never further outstretched between past and future than now.

THE DANGERS OF LONGING

Longing is discredited for many people because they only see the dangers. Such a comprehensive feeling cannot be without dangers either. If longing looks backwards rather than forwards, it leads to a sadly beautiful paralysis as expressed, both seductively and repulsively, in the art of such periods of decadence as Hellenism. If it is directed more to the future than to the past, it brings about restlessness and turbulence, as is characteristic of an age believing in science where everything is happening. Exhilarating longing, on the other hand, exists at the absolute centre of tension between no longer and not yet. It signifies strength from all times within the energy focus of the present. Love is also 'no longer love' and 'not yet love'. Past and future offset each other at the point of tension between the two.

It is clear that backward-looking longing, vainly seeking the mother and father in the beloved, nourishes feelings of being unloved. It is also understandable that forward-looking yearning, measuring the partner against some future ideal, does so too. But how can existential longing – vital excitement within the intensively experienced moment – arouse the same feelings in us?

An answer may perhaps be found in what is known as the *fragment* in literature and the visual arts. Ever since the end of the nineteenth century, the fragment, the torso, the ruin, the unfinished, have acquired a new value as an expression of the fact that there does not exist any absolutely final word, any unconditional 'Yes' or 'No'. A 'Yes' throws the shadow of 'No', and love the shadow of absence of love. With that insight Romanticism prepared the way for depth psychology.

What is the reason for that? As already mentioned, love also signifies yearning, which extends to the past and future. The profundity of our own life story – past and future, origins and objectives – is also involved in love. What brings us closer to these temporal dimensions? *Premonition and memory*, as the Romantics said. Neither can transmit clear-cut truths. Longing is aware of the illusion involved in attempts at unambiguous definition of what is past and what is to come. The remembered past is an illusion, and so too is the foreshadowed future. We can therefore only create fragments with premonition and memory. Childhood memories, said Freud later, are falsifications of some past event which only becomes accessible through falsification. Symbolic images, adds Jung, are also conceptually incomprehensible depictions of objectives. I believe we must go even further. Freud and Jung still regarded the present situation as a real point of reference, but it is merely the point of intersection of what is past and what is to come, and thus of illusions. It is not an autonomous temporal category.

What we create *now* is an incomplete work composed of memories and premonitions. The ruin, torso, fragment and the unfinished relate to the present rather than to the past and the future. The fragment is an *impulse* that falls back to its starting-point, as Novalis explains in his *Theory of the Fragment*. Between an illusory past and an illusory future, the present moment can only be illusory and *enchanting*. 'I'm holding you', says the lover in his enchantment, 'but am I holding *you*? And am *I* holding you? And am I *holding* you?' It is in the very situation of the most intensive experiencing of love that radical questions, which we normally tread underfoot, become perceptible out of the depths of our being: 'I love you. Do I love you? You love me. Do you love me? *Am I loved*?' Such questions involve something much more fundamental than the problem of projection: the unavoidable insufficiency of all words in the grasping of the flow of reality with its constant changes of perspective. After all, every word is magical, attempting to grasp what is flowing. The experience of love, however, dissolves this word-magic and discharges into uncertainty. Longing thus comes into being alongside love, and uncertainty about love together with this yearning. The wound of being unloved opens up at the same time as love.

We don't have any firm ground under our feet so long as we stay in the same place. There do not exist any immutable conditions on which we can base our thoughts and actions, any 'condition of possibility' as Kant says. Our identity is to be found in yearning, in that complex amalgam of feelings concerning reality and illusion, and in that vital impulse which cannot be more closely defined. Depth psychology must draw the consequences of what philosophy has increasingly clearly delineated for over a century now. Only when it relativises its own views, comprehending them merely as perspectives, do people today feel understood by psychology. The healing it transmits otherwise covers up their lack of security. It must also become a radical depth psychology incorporating movement – a form of psycho-energetics.

'The intellect wants to become master of the contradictions of growth and decay'.[1] That is an important psychological statement. As soon as all the means of conceptualisation at our disposal lose contact with the ever-changing nature of reality, they usurp vitality and repulse love. But knowledge must not disregard love. Love knows the most important thing about knowledge – namely that it does not grasp anything solid. All perspectives are displaced for lovers. They don't know 'what is above and what below'. The long-sanctioned feud between the families of Romeo and Juliet becomes nothing but a point of view for the two lovers. How could they love one another otherwise? A supposedly unchanging reality only signifies one possible way of looking at things. Viewed ironically, love has an epistemological value.

The title of this chapter is '*Identity* in longing'. After what has been said, don't the words 'identity' and 'longing' entail a contradiction? Doesn't identity strive for a *fixed* personality whereas longing encourages a *flexible* personality? We want to investigate that apparent contradiction, and thereby finally break through to another explanation of our feelings of being unloved.

Developmental psychology does not see any contradictions in the original predisposition of the individual due to unfold. Such contradictions are viewed as arising in the confrontation with society. Out of that there arises the individual's identity. There is no place in this model for longing as an expression of an essential uncertainty and lack of fulfilment within the individual, apart from the compromise reached with society.

CONCEPT OF IDENTITY

The concept of identity was introduced by Erik Erikson, who studied child development within social structures. Two aspects are involved: 'an inner aspect directed towards structuring and strengthening the self . . . and an outer aspect where the individual is embedded in a social group and at the same time distinguished from it.' The structured self – that is, the identity – is formed out of predisposed potential as also expounded by Heinz Kohut in his theory of narcissism: *'Identity becomes the upholder of the self'*[2] because it attempts to support the greatest possible degree of individuality within a given social structure. For Lichtenstein identity is 'a primary organisational principle without which the process of developmental differentiation could not get under way'.[3] It thus serves the continuity of self-experiencing. Schizophrenic patients are afraid of the opposite: fragmentation of the self through change (Kohut). Primary identity is *'a fundamental structure which remains unchanged as a core guaranteeing personal integrity'*.[4]

The model of identity within developmental psychology summarised there presupposes an individual core whose unfolding can only be obstructed by external factors. For those who think like that, ego-strength is the basis for all further development.

How remote that approach – speaking of upholding, fixity, and guaranteeing the self and its fundamental structure – is from the perspectival language of movement, largely characterising literature and philosophy today! Do our age's intellectual trends, expressed in a language of movement, merely signify dissolution and decadence from which practical psychotherapy, concerned with the sufferings of the tangible individual, must preserve us, or do they simply speak another language? The latter is the case. In the language used they accord with the Buddha when he talks about holding onto nothing and calling nothing his own. In psychological terms, he views structures of personality as auxiliary constructs devised by our intellect to further the object of a fictitious identity. Buddha was nevertheless what I would call a human being with ego-strength. How is that contradiction to be explained? Could it be that he ultimately reached the later one-sided view of a reality in flux on the basis of a solidly founded ego? That would be too simple, even misguided, an answer since it remains within our perspective. So let's try and change the perspective. A language that constantly speaks of structure, an unchanging core, and a guarantee of unity, is an objectifying, static language, abstracting from the subject's experience of movement.

FIRMNESS VS RIGIDITY

Abstraction from movement itself with regard to the 'core' of our personality is unpsychological – that is, it excludes an important psychological factor. A simple example. Firmness in the body, comprehended as lack of movement, is stiffness. The muscles are cramped in an anxious defensive stance. If under attack, an unmovable, firm body is inflexible, that is, weak. A healthy body, on the other hand, moves constantly. Its 'firmness' entails powerful movement. So if 'firmness' is related to activities – for example, to getting stuck in and persisting – it signifies strength. But when related to states – as in the sentence 'I'm firmly convinced' – it betrays weakness. To be firmly rooted in life is only a virtue if that means going through life forcefully but circumspectly. Otherwise it becomes rigidity. The vocabulary of developmental psychology does not pay sufficient attention to the experience of movement in the facts described. This is shaped by a one-sidedly reifying scientific ideal from the past. It is not enough to talk of 'the unfolding of structures from a given potential' and of 'flexible structures'. As long as we establish fixed points of reference, we are abstracting from reality.

The insights of developmental psychology certainly can be transcribed into a language of movement. Just pay attention to the words a child employs while 'grown up' psychologists speak of a 'fixed character structure'. After having lost a game where its ego strength takes a beating, the child will perhaps say: 'I want to *carry on*' – despite the insult suffered. A child uses *doing* words more frequently whilst adults utilise nouns and adjectives when a verb would be appropriate.

From the perspective of movement psychology, it is not contradictory to speak of *identity in longing* (in a flowing psychological state) since the yearning for love mediates a feeling for what developmental psychology's structural language calls the unchanging core of the personality and fundamental identity. The expression 'core of the personality' does not derive from any experience but is the construct of an abstraction. A 'core's' firmness is rather the firmness of a continuum of movement, of a life fully consummated. Tranquillity derives from the psyche's dynamic firmness.

In France Jacques Lacan has contributed towards reformulation of psychoanalysis. That led to a description of human identity where uncertainty, unfamiliarity, insecurity, and suspenseful longing cannot be eliminated since they make man what he is. Lacan's first psychological publication was *The Mirror Stage as Creator of the Ego-Function*.

> From the sixth to the eighteenth month of its life, the child demonstrates a reaction to its mirror-image that differs enormously from that of any other creature – such as a chimpanzee. The chimpanzee loses interest in this mirror-image once it has recognised this is an *image*. The child, on the other hand, rejoices if it recognises that this image is its own reflection.[5]

Lacan derives the genesis of the ego from that fact. At that time the child is still completely dependent and helpless in terms of motor activity since it is, after all, biologically premature. Its visual perception is far more developed than the motor function. A child can therefore recognise the unity of an image much earlier than it can establish the oneness of its own body through motor activity. That is why even an adult finds it easier to recognise the unity of his or her own image optically and intellectually and to perceive the unity of the organism in natural movement. I have observed that people who suddenly became very ill look at themselves in the mirror more frequently than usual so as at least to grasp visually the sense of bodily oneness they have lost. Lacan believes that the process involved in the mirror stage is repeated time and again within adult existence, and I think this mainly happens during periods of crisis. Inhibitions about including the body in analytical work can perhaps be explained by the fact that visual perception of one's own unity predates the inner sense of the oneness of life-processes within the organism. That is why understanding precedes sensing in the thematic arrangement of this book.

WHAT IS A MIRROR IMAGE?

Lacan stresses that a child's jubilation at the sight of itself in a mirror establishes its identity for the first time rather than confirming something that already exists. The child becomes identical with itself in registering its image. But what constitutes this mirror image? Does it look like the child? Is the child's first experience of identity therefore something consistent, an absolute certainty? In his answer Lacan differs from developmental psychology, which takes as its starting point an unchanging core within the child and situates conflicts in socialisation. *'The image is different, heterogeneous with regard to the child'* – not just because of the reversed symmetry but mainly because the image's decisive attributes (unity, fixity, and permanence) are experienced by the child as being absent in its own body.[6] To the ego the image seems fictitious, illusory, and alienating because it leads to identity with something unfamiliar.

The same process repeats itself time and again in adult life. We initially become strangers to ourselves through self-perception, whether that be in a reflection of oneself or – as is also more usual with children – in the image of another person who is unconsciously seen as one's own reflection. We experience ourselves as being *inadequate*. *'I is another'* says Lacan, and thus I will always remain another. The image is not the representation of a reality we know about from somewhere else. What is depicted in the image only *is* through being thus represented. We are an endless reflection.

Now what feeling is central and primal, according with this endless reflection? *Longing!* We long for the other we are. Lacan speaks of the 'désir de l'autre', the 'longing for the other'. The French word 'désir' means craving and desire as well as longing. Our identity primarily exists in longing for the other we are, not in a compromise between disposition and society. We ourselves are this state of tension involving the other. All knowledge about ourselves and the world is mediated by way of this tension towards the other with which we are identical.

I believe that we can also comprehend anew what Jung called the *'shadow'* against the background of Lacan's views on the mirror stage. For Lacan the other is not *inside* ourselves as something unfamiliar within what is known. It is not a dark aspect of the personality alongside the light that we know. We become aware of the 'shadow', the 'double', in the never to be fulfilled longing for ourselves. It is always other, and we are other. From that perspective, there does not exist any 'integration of the shadow', which Jung considered to be an objective within human maturation. Since we do not have any fixed point of reference within ourselves 'integration of the shadow', 'the assumption of a dark inner personality', and psychological progress in general are, viewed radically, an illusion. The fundamental longing for the other remains, even when we have made conscious and 'integrated' in our life much that was previously unconscious. That burns within us just as much as at the time when we 'beginners' were even less 'advanced'. The obverse of this longing is *alienation* (Albert Camus) and *strangeness*: the unfathomable feeling of not being 'loved'. We feel secure and loved to the degree that we recognise ourselves in the other. If, however, the other disconcerts us, we feel estranged and unloved. The wound of being unloved is particularly painful when launching forth into a new phase of life. We then strive to know anew the other we are because its strangeness is so painful. However, I'll show in chapter 15 that the other awakens love in ourselves as well as being painful.

I have been concerned for years, in a variety of contexts, with perception of the self in the mirror image of the other. I initially called that 'mirror communication'[7] and then 'model reflection'.[8]

Adults also perceive themselves in the other – just like a child rejoices to recognise its wholeness . nd oneness in a real mirror, and also figuratively in someone closely related. The relationship to another involved in the sensation of love initially arouses the satisfying feeling of attunement and security. We breathe a sigh of relief, having come at last from alienation into what is our own. The images two people exchange awaken in each the experience of coming 'to themselves'. This doesn't involve projections but mirror images where both the reflector and the reflected recognise themselves. Love is thus a celebratory encounter between what the other perceives in me and needs for his or her life, and what I perceive in the other and need for my existence. Viewed on that level, there occurs a wonderful incorporation of the other into one's own life. The other is 'an image of my secret life'. If, for instance, I used to be a somewhat reserved person, I have now become more open through inner perception of the other. The perception itself transformed me. In the other I am fascinated by the very thing which is now awaiting development within myself. At the right moment the model reflection provided by the person loved awakens one's own vital potential. Only love can dissolve resistance to an appropriate step forwards. Love is the energy in the reflection of a model. That reflection of a model can be summarised in these steps:

1. The love energy will be attracted by you as the mirror image of my hidden self. Aspects of your personality, now of importance for my own development, are occupied by this energy. I experience that occupation as interest and fascination, which are often intermingled with rejection and sometimes even complete aversion. If the latter is the case, aversion must be transformed into attraction through coming to terms with whatever repels.
2. The love energy returns as a mirror image from you to me as something reflected, vitalising within my living potential corresponding and hitherto unconscious aspects of personality.

3.   Stimulation of those aspects of personality initiates a new way
     of living into which the reflected flows.

The first two steps occur of their own accord if two people
love one another. The third and decisive step, however, is
the outcome of becoming conscious of the first two and
then taking a deliberate decision. This reflection of a model
generates a *cycle of love energy* between two people. I have
described that in detail in my book *How to Say No to the One
You Love (Das Nein in der Liebe)*.

Longing persists, no matter in what stage of a love relationship we may be. Why? The first answer is easy to understand.
The other still has a lot to tell me about himself or herself. I
long to enjoy to the full his or her essence within myself, and
I long for recreation of my life. The second answer is more
profound. Despite all the closeness of our love, I remain
remote from myself and yourself because I *am* the other,
and don't therefore ever reach me or you. During periods of
upheaval we particularly notice that it isn't only details that
change. Life as a whole is different. One day I awaken from
the illusion of peaceful continuity and realise that everything
familiar has been taken away from me. *Everything is different.*
The partnership is different, the light and the world are different. I am the other. From the perspective of this fundamental
experience, there is no development. Any linear progress in a
chain of causes and effects is self-deception. In moving only
the movement is real 'You've gone far', people sometimes say
to a person who has proceded further than they. But in the
moment they say that, there perhaps no longer exists for the
other any 'very far' or 'less far'.

AFRAID OF THE OTHER

As long as two people who love one another live out of the
consciousness of how much or how little each of them had
already progressed thanks to the relationship, they are living
a lie. Contact with the other, who is simply other, is still
lacking. They want to 'integrate' one another and suppress
the essential yearning. They count out the steps they have
taken as if it were a matter of checking children's homework.
They are afraid of the other, the unfamiliar, and the uncertain.

They avoid the tension of longing, which brings to mind the 'no longer' and the 'not yet', and anaesthetise the wound of being unloved. Yet one day, perhaps in a sudden crisis, all the steps that have been taken return at top speed to the very beginning, just like a long line of dominoes toppled by a single push.

That is awakening. Objectives and the realisation of life plans are no longer at issue. We can now encounter one another at a silent depth where each is other and unfamiliar. The reflection of the model no longer occurs in a comprehensible succession of images but within insatiable longing between reflections.

PART THREE

Sensing

NINE

Pressure and Impulse

We are on the threshold of a new sensing. Defensive feelings directed during the painful sixties and seventies against coldness, brutality, and the mechanisms of economic, technological, and political power are gradually yielding to active sensing of the self in discovery of the living body and the living environment. The Frankfurt School, whose main exponent was Adorno, was characterised by extreme psychological sensitivity bordering on nausea.[1] A feeling of happiness was utopian in the life of those who had to suffer from the omnipresent principle of dominance. 'Politically and psychologically, the aesthetic theory of "sensitivity" was founded on an attitude of reproach, compounded of suffering, contempt, and rage, against everything that possessed power'.[2] Viewed psycho-energetically, this was a reaction to external affliction, to external *pressure*. It was a theory of sensing fixated on external manifestations of power.

Those in the post war generation who felt they'd had a raw deal and been unloved suffered from resentment, the narcissism of a constantly bleeding wound. Today increasingly many 'sensitive' contemporaries feel the wound of being unloved can be productive. It spurs on the inner *impulse towards pleasurable sensing*.

That gives rise to the task of transforming outer pressure into inner impulse, and releasing the vitality of energy frozen in defensive attitudes. The unloved are of exemplary significance in therapeutic practice. Their conscious turning away from oppression towards liberation is also of social relevance. They are among the protagonists on the by no means self-evident way towards a primal vitality. The turning point involved was symbolically demonstrated in 1969, not long before Adorno died, when a group of demonstrators prevented the philosopher from lecturing and female students bared their breasts in front of him. The naked flesh demanded its rights. 'It was the power of nakedness, not naked power, that silenced the philosopher'.[3] The nakedness then demonstratively displayed today starts to reveal its purpose in the self-uncovering of the vitality seeking expression. The body is awakening, and with it sensitivity to the wounded environment. Nothing is more urgently needed today than a body *sensitive to the world*.

Love does not exist without the capacity for physical sensing. The unloved need the development of their capacity for sensing so as to be able to love themselves. I call the vitality sensed within oneself, seeking expression, an *inner impulse*. The pages that follow are concerned with its liberation, and thus the liberation of love energy.

CIVILISATION'S VICTIMS

People who feel themselves unloved are always downcast, sad, and worried, so any kind of 'pressure therapy' is inappropriate for them. As 'civilisation's victims' they constitute closed energy-systems, and therefore experience every form of external influence as pressure. They have a justified dislike of fixed philosophies of life which lay claim to being able to heal. They experience such ideologies as a restriction and lack of love, as a betrayal of feeling and sensing reality. Anyone who exerts external pressure on others removes himself from their inner life, and it is that chilly distancing which is reminiscent of the early wound of being unloved. The *Apollonian principle* of orderly development, which Nietzsche calls the 'principium individuationis', is suspected of involving subordination to a system. In his radiance, the moderate, delimited, and distanced Apollo seems to be mere appearance, and his incandescent beauty serves to eliminate what is wild, inward, and immediately experienced and felt – in other words, the *Dionysian principle*. Pretensions to harmony are suspected of insidious violation.

Ever since Nietzsche, distrusting reactions to Apollo have shaped cultural history. Separation from Dionysos has alienated the Apollonian principle from its origins, making it destructive. That is not put to rights by theorising about the links between Apollo and Dionysos, order and chaos, impulsive wildness and restrained structuring. This link can only be comprehended in terms of the dynamics of both poles. Dionysos is the original, comprehensive principle. Apollo is not equally endowed. The god Dionysos is the god of completeness – of both Thracian and Greek, man and woman – simultaneously wild and civilised. Integrative wholeness constitutes his essence. The moment that Dionysos turns against himself by looking in a mirror, he is undone. The Titans dismember him.

Apollo embodies one half of Dionysos, striving for luminosity, order, and harmony. His gift for prophesy also derives from Dionysos, without whom Apollo loses his profound knowledge, just as a human being alienated from physical sensing loses any capacity for deeper insight and more comprehensive wisdom. Norms only take on meaning in conjunction with unnormed vitality, order only in connection with creative chaos, and intellectuality only in association with the body. Anyone who has forgotten the impulse towards birth has succumbed to death. People who think the body out of existence think against life. They lose intellectual spontaneity together with bodily mobility. They confuse vitality and compulsively pursued chains of ideas and over-valued concepts whose substitute character they do not recognise. They exude lack of pleasure because only true self-expression generates pleasure: delight in vital impulse and fresh birth. The Apollonian principle of intellectuality needs constant awareness of its origins in the Dionysian principle of intensity forcing a way into life so that sovereign clarity – as, for instance, manifested in the statue of Apollo in the Temple of Zeus on Mount Olympus – doesn't become aloof narrow-mindedness. I'll pursue Apollo and Dionysos further in the following chapter.

Psycho-energetics re-invests the Dionysian principle with its original significance. Without that we feel that much of what we do is in response to external demands and external pressure, which exhausts our energy. Our task is to become absolutely one with the intensity of the life struggling for expression. Everything that exists within ourselves wishes to be included there. Dionysos is absolute affirmation, even of such unchangeable negations as an unhappy childhood, separation, loss, illness, death, and all the pains entailed in growth. If we adopt an attitude of extensive affirmation, we do not run the risk of the impulse towards life becoming external pressure in testing situations, or of creative gestures becoming defensive. What a load falls away when we are no longer victims of alien forces but act out of our own strength. How light and mobile we suddenly become! Life pours out of us. We have withdrawn our energy from defence of a facade, and liberated ourselves from oppression. A new joyousness proliferates. We will no longer be assailed by alien misfortune. If we do experience misfortune, it is our own as an expression of our lust for life even amid the darkness.

From time to time most people reach a point where things become 'simply too much' with the vital impulse transformed into distress, and delight in life into listlessness resulting from psychological pressure. Some time or other we come unstuck and have had it up to here. As those familiar phrases show, we experience that sudden change from the still supportable to the unbearable, from impulse to pressure, as almost an expression of destiny. 'I've long been able to accept everything, but now I'm overwhelmed', someone might say at a difficult stage in their life. Will he at long last let his suffering and tearful lamentation take its course? If so, his impulse towards life will find appropriate expression in dark times. He no longer closes himself to the pain and torment of which his life at present consists. Or does the proclamation 'I'm overwhelmed' signify: 'Something alien, which has nothing to do with me, and with which I don't want to be involved, is overcoming me'? In that case he seeks to apportion guilt: his parents, his partner, God, or himself. The longer he laments or accuses, the more dejected he becomes and the more he burdens himself with other people's or his own guilt.

Isn't it natural that from a specific moment onwards things simply become too much for us, the vital impulse falters, and something all-powerful oppresses in both painful and pleasurable situations? There is only an indirect answer to that. We can always shift the point where the impulse turns into pressure, and affirmation into anxiety. We can *carry on*, even from the place where we have always stopped, and *go further* than ever before. Dionysos is stronger than we think possible.

IMPULSE AND PRESSURE

The crucial aspect in every moment entails remaining within the impulse. We no longer need interrupt the 'flow of power and meaning', either in vital conversations, or in passionate embraces and self-oblivious dancing, or even in pain and suffering.[4] The intensity of the pressure to which we are now exposed reveals the intensity of the impulse wanting to free itself. I have the same experience (albeit varying in degree) with all of my clients. The moment when impulse becomes pressure can be delayed, sometimes to such an extent that it doesn't even occur on some days. The therapist's persistent attentiveness creates the precondition for the client always going somewhat further than he otherwise would. This enables steps forward that were not possible in the vacuum of isolation. The therapist is a sympathetic observer of what must happen, particularly in situations where previously closely related figures turned away and no longer wanted to bear witness.

This process does not involve a strengthening of the *toleration of frustration* in psycho-analytical terms, entailing improvement of our capacity to withstand pressure. The experience of pressure is taken there as an established fact. When subject to difficulties, we learn to grit our teeth and keep going despite everything. Psycho-energetics, on the other hand, is concerned with transforming pressure into impulse. Even when we experience illness, we do not need to submit. What is at issue is to remain within the life that remains to us rather than anticipating death. In this fundamentally Dionysian attitude of flowing emotional identity, we even experience – in some mysterious and profound way – ignominy and pain as pleasure, essentially differing little from merriment, an embrace, and devotion. Nothing remains here of Freud's stoical view that: 'Enduring life nevertheless remains the prime duty for anyone alive'.[5] Life as duty is life as pressure to which man must submit. The pleasure principle must yield to the reality principle. The energy principle, however, which exists under the sign of

Dionysos, unites both in affirming a life that we no longer divide by passing judgements. No matter how important it may be to avoid pain, it is just as necessary to become one with suffering if it is unavoidable and now determines our life.

Ever since an illness brought me to the brink of death at the beginning of 1985, I pause during situations when I am under pressure, sometimes intensely feeling that 'I'm alive'. That isn't saying that 'I'm alive *despite* the stress' but rather 'I'm alive in that stress, and am identical with it. My life pulses in that stress, and I no longer pass judgement'. That feeling is profoundly and incomparably pleasurable. Must I add that it in no way involves fatalism let alone masochism, but directs life in the best direction possible? As long as a distinction is made between pleasure and something contrary, that is not the pleasure of Dionysos.

The unloved quickly feel under pressure. That is why they set their sights too low. A short dialogue by Confucius illustrates that. A disciple, Ran Qin, declares: 'It's not that I don't find the Master's way excellent, but I lack the necessary strength'. To which Confucius answered: 'Those who lack strength sink to the ground, exhausted, halfway to their goal. You establish your limits in advance'.[6] Ran Qin puts himself under pressure to achieve, and comes to a stop, discouraged. The Master senses the vitality hidden from the disciple himself. His answer is intended to transform pressure on the pupil into a pleasurable impulse. That is healing through relationship.

A younger man told me about a critical behavioural pattern. 'When I meet a woman who pleases me, I only persist until I see: "It's working out. She's interested in me". That's enough for me. I always break off at that point. And I do the same in my studies. As soon as I begin to understand a problem, it doesn't interest me any longer. The outcome is that up to now I've never established a relationship or passed an examination'. This young man didn't allow himself the pleasure of a movement carried through to its natural conclusion. Who was the resentful figure, the secret oppressor? The image of his mother, telling him: 'I never made it in my life either. Be a good son to me and go the same way as I did!' He thus satisfied himself with mere gestures, saying that he could basically do whatever it was, cheating himself of the pleasure of actually doing so.

Some people's lives are no more than a hint of what is possible. The impulse remains symbolic, and the pressure real. Pressure creates anxiety, and anxiety confines life. The Indo-Germanic word 'angh' is the German 'eng' meaning cramped and confined. Anxiety is the constriction with which we oppress ourselves.

The unloved, trapped in their childhood, often reproach their partner with something that they in fact experienced from their parents. For instance, 'You put me under pressure so that I fit in with you. If I don't do that, you run away'. But the danger of the partner running away is less than the unloved fear. And if he or she does, then the person left is no longer the child dependent on its parents. No one must become a slave through conforming.

The opposite happens too. The unloved sometimes become tyrants by not conforming because they confuse empathy with subordination, and renunciation of a one-sided point of view with submission. In both cases – enslavement through conformity, and tyranny through failure to adapt – what is missing is the naturalness of a love capable of breaking the chains of childhood experience. *Collusion*[7] frequently occurs between a *slave* to *conformity* and a *tyrant of non-adaptation*. It is then salutary to uncover the power-free realm of a mutual vibration, and consciously extend that. A woman, who had been a slave of conformity ever since her childhood, started making music for an hour every day with her husband, a tyrant of non-adaptation. In music they experienced one another working together. They were not fixated on one another but rather jointly concerned with the music they were producing. The experience of resonance marked the beginnings of understanding for both of them. The impulse for life in the one thus awoke a similar impulse – rather than counter-pressure – in the other until both were united in shared striving. What a wonderful discovery!

I don't know any more apt passage in literature about that 'going further' which prevents a predicament from being transformed into paralysing pressure than van Leyden's monologue during feverish delirium in Sloterdijk's book *The Magic Tree*. Here's a taste of that:

This dreadfully determined life which doesn't give up so easily . . . eating its way through the wall like a patient battering-ram of a plant . . . It sucks from the stones what it needs to survive the next moment – and then you will see what happens after that. You will attempt something else so as to try out whether that might suffice for yet another moment . . . and another, perhaps the last . . . But don't give up . . . This expression of vitality starts singing softly, and crowing. It uses the tiny dying voice like a chisel in order to bore its way into the wall . . . You must carry on singing, you must continue making this cave with your voice – boring and boring. Nothing else takes your life a step further. The voice must remain since you are the voice.[8]

To go further is to *carry on singing* – the resounding, vibrating persistence of what is alive. That isn't a metaphor. Someone depressed and under stress really does suffer a loss of vibration. His voice loses fullness and depth, and his emotions and feelings become shallow.[9] If we react to stressful situations by resolutely singing and humming, we will perhaps regain a sense of ourself. 'Singing is for convalescents'.[10] It's well known that people who are afraid in the dark spontaneously start whistling or singing. That increases their courage. The succession of notes provides a sense of the flow of life. A man told me that he always used to feel under stress and pressure during long car trips. Once, when he happened to be in a particularly good mood, he warbled away to himself, sometimes quietly sometimes more loudly, for the whole of a six hour trip. When the journey was over, he felt fresh and relaxed. Anyone who sings breathes in deeply and out slowly. Previously the car driver had obviously breathed shallowly and nervously, thereby losing feeling for the streaming of his vital energy.

IMPORTANCE OF EYE CONTACT

Intensive *eye contact* also makes the unloved – people who during childhood didn't learn trust in relationships – feel under pressure. They lose touch with themselves. Their vitality congeals. I mentioned that in connection with the unloved game 'Always a little too late'. During breast feeding a baby looks up regularly so as to establish eye contact with the mother.[11] If a child later loses trust in its parents, it quickly looks away. The child is afraid they will interfere with its own existence. From that time onwards the child lacks encouragement in its own impulse towards life. The parents' demanding or distant gaze is felt to disturb its well-being, and is avoided. Adults who as children had to isolate themselves in this fashion initially associate any relationship with pressure. That is why the unloved are so hesitant about relationships. The living energy in their eyes regularly subsides. Their look loses its alluring vitality, becoming glassy and hard so that other people's gaze is dashed to pieces there rather than penetrating.

Another man reported that at the age of eleven he bought a thriller because its title, *The Woman in the Glass Coffin*, fascinated him. Ever since his childhood, his own vitality had been locked up as if in a glass coffin. When someone looked at him, he felt constrained and couldn't turn away no matter how much he tried. His eyes became glass behind which he was dying. Delight and vitality vanished when he was subject to the hypnosis of an unfamiliar gaze. His *compulsive look* simultaneously demonstrated a loss of autonomy and vitality, and the need of relationship. Spontaneity is usually only possible during brief eye contact. Only during intensive shared experiences of love and affinity do two people maintain vital eye contact for longer periods. A pleasurable arousal takes hold of lovers, who look at each other steadfastly.

In every moment of life there is an optimal tension, which we should not underplay or exceed. The latter is also possible. We can go too far. An unloved person sometimes heroically overestimates himself, seeks refuge in attack, and overdoes things. 'Draw (the bow) to the limit, and you will wish you had stopped in time' (Lao Tse). Pressure is not transformed into impulse, zest, and joy in life. Instead all possible strength is summoned up for a violent breakthrough. That's a tragedy. Such people destroy themselves on the ice they cannot melt in their hearts. They destroy what they wanted to caress. The following declaration by Nietzsche also applies to the author himself. 'Men of profound sadness betray themselves when they are happy. They have a way of seizing happiness as if they would like to crush and smother it'.[12] Even in the heroically-inclined unloved, inhibitions are stronger than inclination, pressure than impulse.

This chapter has been concerned with elucidation of the Dionysian attitude to pleasure, which transforms what oppresses us into autonomous, urgent vitality. We thereby gain an affirmatory attitude even towards activities we previously assessed negatively. In Mark Twain's novel *The Adventures of Tom Sawyer* the hero persuades his friend Huckleberry Finn to change his views in such a way. Tom convinces Huck that it would be great fun to paint Aunt Polly's fence. Tom himself got out of this unpleasant obligation whilst his friend did the same work with the greatest of pleasure. Tom's pressure became Huck's impulse. What appears in this novel as a useful suggestion becomes in the Dionysian attitude a comprehensive affirmation of reality, testifying to unqualified realism.

TEN

The Word Becomes Flesh

BODILY SPIRITUALITY

In January 1987 I walked for an hour from the South Indian
village of Alagatovil to visit a temple dedicated to the
monkey deity Hanuman, a manifestation of the god Shiva
emanating vitality and wisdom. Like Dionysos in Ancient
Greece, Shiva is India's god of the dance and ecstasy,
dissolving all fixed forms and ideas in a single dance of
creation and destruction. His element is fire as a symbol
of energy. Visitors entering Hanuman's shrine undergo a
baptism of fire. They pass their hands through a flame
burning in a bowl held by a priest. They then rub these
blackened hands over their face. Finally the priest marks
their forehead with red and white powder, the colours of
creation and destruction. After this baptism of fire, visitors
descend into a grotto where there is a bubbling spring. Here
they are abundantly sprinkled with water by an assistant to
the priest. Life is transformed into water and flows without
restriction, thanks to the circulation of energy involved in
creation and destruction.

When I had left the temple and was passing through a
wood, I encountered, coming from the other direction, a
wildly ecstatic throng of young priests of Shiva, dancing,
jumping, singing religious songs, and beating tambourines.
I had just participated with great interest – but more or less as
a spectator – in the temple fire and water rites, but now all of a
sudden I was enchanted and caught up in a whirlpool of life
and movement. My reflections on the symbolic significance
of what I had seen at the temple evaporated, dissolving in
the Shiva acolytes' rhythmic dance movements. As soon as
the *symbols* vanished as visual images, they began to live.

They were transformed into all-embracing gestures within the central focus of the movement with which they became identical. The dance steps, extreme contortions, self-forgetful and penetrating singing, and vibrant rhythms unfolded out into the world with the logical consistency of unrestricted growth. Never before had I seen such congruence of freely pulsating life and ritual process, of nature and culture. What was most personal and inward was awoken and impelled within this rite. From a distance these men seemed like a noisy, boisterous, and totally 'freaked out' crowd, which might perhaps be dangerous for an outsider who didn't go along with them. Viewed from nearby, an ancient archetypal rite, rooted deep within man, became manifest. I sensed how much we Westerners lack such rites. In Christianity rituals have either vanished or largely petrified as ceremonies followed word for word. Throughout its history the Church has ruthlessly thwarted any attempts at simply celebrating the vitality of what is alive. It wanted to preserve order but lost that as well. We owe to the influence of pagan antiquity the fact that sensuousness nevertheless erupts into Christian art. This sensuousness has to justify its existence within Christianity by adding a gesture of suffering in the sadly beautiful depictions of the Man of Sorrows, Our Lady of Sorrows, the penitent sinner Mary Magdalene, Sebastian impaled by arrows, and other martyrs.

DANCING DERVISHES

Where in Christianity are the dancing dervishes whose esctatic circlings liberate them from all artificially fixed ideas, from virtue and vice? The medieval St. Vitus' dancers moving from town to town, orgiastic Dionysian zealots in whom we recognise Greek Bacchantic choruses, have long since vanished. The St. Vitus' dance was ultimately downgraded as a pathological symptom within a group of illnesses entailing motor disturbances.

In *The Birth of Tragedy* Nietzsche evokes lost Dionysian oneness: 'Man is no longer an artist. He has become a work of art. The artistic dynamism of the whole of nature manifests itself here amid shudders of intoxication – to the great delight and satisfaction of the primordial one'. The artist turns into the work of art, man into his actions, and the symbol into gestures. Depth psychology also had to devote itself directly to this deeply moving and profoundly transforming experience. It is impossible to describe such an experience with professorial detachment. If it is to be understood it must be consummated. Among depth psychologists, perception of the corporeal all too seldom becomes an event leading to insight and physical thinking. That explains their lack of sensitivity to environment and cosmos. Depth psychology has still not sufficiently followed up thoughts expressed by C. G. Jung in a 1928 lecture.

> The body lays claim to equal recognition; it exerts the same fascination as the psyche. If we are still caught in the old idea of an antithesis between mind and matter, this state of affairs must seem like an unbearable contradiction. But if we can reconcile ourselves to the mysterious truth that the spirit is the life of the body seen from within, and the body the outward manifestation of the spirit – the two being really one – then we can understand why the striving to transcend the present level of consciousness through acceptance of the unconscious must give the body its due, and why recognition of the body cannot tolerate a philosophy that denies it in the name of the spirit.[1]

Jung himself approaches the experience of the symbol at work in the gesture. For him spiritual development rightly signifies the individual becoming open and alert to the accessible archetypes – that is, to the developmental pattern connecting all human beings. He called that *individuation* in order to distinguish it from blind conformity to the spirit of the collective. Would it not be more meaningful – from the point of view of depth psychology – to call that *participation*: conscious participation by the individual in the collective unconscious (the potential for human development) rather than the alienating collective spirit? Calling spiritual development participation entails renunciation of the observer keeping his distance from reality and instead grasping human existence as participatory action. Primal images' only function is to lure us towards the primal gestures common to everyone.

Let us, for instance, imagine the primal image of the mother

and child. Perhaps we are moved, feeling touched by the idea
of feeding, caring, and security. But so long as the image is
there for our contemplation, a certain distance exists between
it and ourselves. It doesn't transform us sufficiently. So let's go
further! Let's not exclude coming into physical contact with it!
Let's become one with its dynamism! Now we have opened
ourselves within our individual being, 'de-individualising'
ourselves through participation in the image's dynamism.
It is only now that the image becomes a developmental
matrix. *Participation* is the essential element within what
Jung called the *individuation* process. As long as the individual persists in his separation, he blocks his own growth. The
image must become a creative gesture. We then transform
ourselves into the mother who gives and the child that receives with the two aspects forming a harmonious unity. The
term individuation suggests miscomprehension of a spiritual
development through separation, which completely contra-
dicts Jung's intention.

TRANSFORMING IMAGES

In the free dance, involving meditative sensing of what
urgently seeks expression, we ourselves become a moving
image and shaping work of art. The fixed image we have
of ourselves is transformed into perception of an unfolding
form: a gesture. In the process we register physically what is
still missing in the image impelling towards self-realisation.
Perhaps we establish that our self-presentation is not forceful
enough, noticing our weight is on the tips of the toes rather
than the heels, so that we are insufficiently linked with the
earth and motherliness, and thus anxious and inhibited like
unloved children. If the symbol is transformed into a gesture,
it becomes binding, linking us with body and world. That
doesn't only happen in the dance. It occurs in every gesture
with which we consciously identify ourselves. Maintaining
a distance when thinking *about* a symbol weakens its vital
strength as a gesture.

'No symbol has genuine being in the soul if it lacks genuine
being in the body' (Martin Buber), that is, if it does not entail
vital consummation of a gesture. Primal images of what is
involved in being human want to dance into our existence.

Our ideas should follow – with cautious reverence – what emerges out of us but never become its representative. The symbol concentrates life-energy in the rhythmic structure of a gesture. What matters is to implement this gesture rightly so that it accords with the prevailing situation. The *energy-conscious human being* living in the flow of his gestures doesn't therefore strive for any objectives since no moment within a gesture is more important than any other. 'What vanity – wanting to penetrate the target when shooting off an arrow. There will always be someone stronger that you. Only the *correctness of the gesture* is important'.[2] (Confucius).

It isn't easy to free the *concept of the symbol* from the *static idea* already present in its linguistic origins. Symbol originally signified a means of identification resulting from the fitting together (Greek – 'symballein') of two fragments of a bowl. Even in its later meaning of a conceptually inexhaustible image, inducing reflection on the object presented – such as a lion standing for power, aggression, and so on – the symbol lacked the mobility of a gesture. If, however, to simplify, we play a lion, forgetting our former identity in powerfully raising the head and roaring sonorously, the symbol of the lion becomes a gesture. The physical being of this symbol in the gestures brings about a conscious experience of aggression and power. The same happens when we alertly live through, rather than simply reflect on, the hitherto repressed and now recovered contents of consciousness, which would be termed symbols in Freud's psychoanalysis.

A *dream symbol* is not a subject for discussion either, but rather a psychological movement entered upon by both partners in the therapeutic discussion, tracking down the emotion and meaning that want to liberate themselves there. The movement in the dream wishes to be continued in the waking stage, not to ossify in reflection. Of course, analysts and other therapists employing words are not experts in movement and dance. But words can also be 'gestures' – of the voice, mood, attunement, and concurrence with what is real. Effective therapy takes place by way of living speech. Conversely, words which are not effective words hinder the therapeutic process. *Effective* words are part of an overall gesture to which bodily stance, movement, emanation, and eye language also belong. Words viewed in that way are thus collective human sound-gestures in which the most subtle experiences of an entire culture vibrate.

Effective words, expressing reality, are therefore linguistic gestures. Like all gestures with which we are identical, they generate *emotion*. They activate life-energy. They suggest, recall and transform us if we open ourselves to them as a sounding space. Abstract words, on the other hand, choke such emotion even if they do mobilise hectic movement. People who hasten to tell you about all and sundry stifle the fundamental sound of their soul. They keep their distance from the sentences and images employed. Here are three examples of how and why people drop out from what they are saying, suppressing emotion, and distancing themselves from the impact of their words.

I asked a man who talked rapidly and a great deal why he often broke off in mid-sentence. His answer ran: 'I'd like to tell you so much more than I can. If I'm talking about last night's dream, I remember what I dreamt the previous night. If I'm telling you about a conversation with my wife, a childhood memory of my mother intervenes and I absolutely want to mention that. I really do have too much imagination'. But of course it wasn't an excess of imagination that silenced this man when he was in full flow. It was the sudden distancing, produced by distrust, from the course taken. We attain the greatest possible degree of completeness in a communication when we are nothing but the relationship to that which we are at present communicating – a unifying gesture, neither doubting nor deviating.

A person's flow of words provides precise information about the flow of life in all aspects of his or her existence. My second example is intended to demonstrate that. I'm thinking of a woman who erupts into speech as if she must force her voice into expression, countering external pressure. Then she tires and her voice loses colour; she struggles helplessly for words, and finally succumbs to a bitter silence. She is one of the unloved who from an early age wanted, by way of surprise attacks, to gain a hearing for herself whilst inwardly knowing she would never succeed.

My third example again involves a man. He's a man of few words, a walking demonstration of the insignificance of one's own words. He hesitantly starts speaking, his voice scarcely to be heard, ready to sink once again into himself at the first sign of conflict. But if he isn't stopped and people even listen to him, he becomes clearer, more resolute and open, pulls himself together, and gains both strength and eloquence until finally everyone hangs onto his every word. During his childhood he was loved excessively vehemently, and could only venture to escape step by tiny step so as to enjoy love in the small doses he was capable of digesting. But he often fell silent since the outer pressure he felt also frustrated the least thing he had to say.

The man in the first example, who suddenly broke off his sentences when talking to me, was as a child time and again interrupted by his parents. If he was playing, it was time to do his homework. If he was busy with such school tasks, his father called him a lazy 'stay at home' and wanted his help in bringing in the hay. If he was doing that, his mother needed him to help peel the potatoes. Later he started interrupting himself. When he abruptly stopped speaking, he revealed himself to be someone unloved. He often accompanied that with a disparaging hand movement, sometimes supplemented by the words: 'That's stupid'. So he viewed what he had to say, what came out of him, what he wanted to set free, as stupid and not worth mentioning! Then, after he had brought his invisible parents the symbolic sacrifice of his supposed stupidity, he could carry on speaking, albeit once again in a great hurry, knowing in advance that he would quickly be interrupted again – that he would interrupt himself.

USING MEMORIES

Childhood memories are not the most important element in analysis of the flow of talk. No direct change is to be expected from such memories. Nevertheless they strengthen and expand sensitivity to current energy processes as what might be viewed as their clarificatory projection onto the screen of the past. I'm sometimes asked: 'I've now gained a sense of all that, but how can I *put it into effect*? How can I *get rid of* this restricting energy-pattern, this dissociation from my own vital gesture?' Anyone who asks that has already once again lost his feeling for the energy-pattern that may perhaps have been briefly sensed. Wanting to put into effect and get rid of entails establishing a distance so as to work on a problem from outside, as setting about a block of marble with a chisel. But that very approach is a contradictory, hopeless enterprise. After all, who has problems? The block of marble or me? And doesn't the problem rather entail the chisel grasped so tightly? It is sufficient to remain *in touch*: receptive, alert, non-self-critical (that is, without splitting off from oneself by way of a negative judgement) – as nothing more than sensitivity to what is happening now so that the old energy pattern melts from within and we find our way to a holistic vital gesture. The decisive factor is to tell oneself: 'I myself am the person who time and again interrupts or brings to silence, choking his natural emotion. He is now my life and therefore of value. Without criticism I am identical with him'. He thus unites with life and is saved from himself.

And there I'm back with Dionysos and Apollo, the often misunderstood pair of gods. From time to time we want to bring some order into our lives, to 'deal with' a problem. We develop a specific idea about what we want to change, and express that in words. That word is supposed to become flesh. We want to transform it into action and restructure it as vitality. Such attempts cannot succeed over the longer term. Order does not develop out of the abstraction of an idea. Apollo, the god of order, is not an intellectual construct. He is contained within and born out of Dionysos, the god of the unrestricted flow of life. What does that entail?

Viewed historically, the Dionysian found its own way to order, initially in establishment of the Greek city states, and later also beyond Greece's frontiers in mystery cult rituals. Psychologically too, the Dionysian, the free flow of vital energy in all spheres, becomes order. Every rhythmic process orders. Life sensed from within involves ordering rhythm (see chapter 4, p.30, the second experience of energy). Anyone who entrusts himself to that energy, remaining alert and conscious, experiences his or her life spontaneously structuring itself. That is why I started this chapter with the dancing priests of Shiva. For the distrustful, standing on the sidelines, such a dance is a chaotic, compulsive letting off of steam, lacking anything spiritual or orderly. But the closer we come to the dancers, and the more we allow ourselves to be drawn into their dance, the more the rhythm – with which we are now identical – becomes a dynamic order and structuring gesture. The structure is born out of the movement of life. 'Flesh' – the bodily and earthly – is not the adversary of the ordering spirit and its expression in the word. If we do not obstruct its vitality, it gives birth to the spirit and the word.

The Christian idea of the word becoming flesh is not aware of its origins in the flesh becoming the word. Meaning arises out of life fulfilling itself, not vice versa. That is a fundamental psychological experience, which does not allow any 'both/and'. External verbal impulses may be able to arouse life within ourselves, but they only do that because those particular words were ready to awaken within us. It isn't an unfamiliar word that becomes flesh within ourselves, but the flesh awakens to its word. The body expresses itself through its spirit. The Christian perspective of the word become flesh, the incarnation, leads of necessity to hostility towards many other words which the flesh should say in order to become radiant and whole. Ideas, confessions of faith, ideologies: the most diverse of 'incarnations' (that is, the word becoming flesh) separate from life spontaneously improvising itself and are a vehicle of power, offering through identification the illusion of belonging to the whole but nonetheless leading to disagreement between individuals and social groupings.

In therapy the changing of the word becoming the flesh into its opposite offers a decisive insight. What do I mean by that? Therapy is initiated with the objective of getting rid of specific troublesome symptoms. That is very understandable. An idea is supposed to be implemented. The client is full of words that 'want to become flesh', striving for implementation. And yet, so long as the preconceived intention determines the way the therapy goes, nothing essential can happen. The client doesn't love himself unconditionally, and is not identical with his reality. From outside he applies an ordering principle to himself – a norm, an objective. The flesh feels itself unloved. The body gets tense when reason subjects itself to so many well-intended contortions. If, however, the client renounces objectives, loves his own flesh and his own body – and his own life as reciprocated in the therapeutic relationship – without preconceived words or any ifs and buts, miracles happen. Symptoms are alleviated or completely vanish, not because they are inconsistent with the norm of psychological health, but because a life that has become warmer and more flowing melts them away of its own accord. A new and natural order of life starts to grow. Existence coins a new language, a new and more liberated form of expression. The flesh has become the word!

Society, like the individual, also needs such 'physicality of thought'. So long as we play off the intellect against the body, and ideas against what is real, we will lack love of the world as a whole and of humanity's fundamental concern. The idea that forces itself on reality destroys that reality's natural dynamism. When the intellect becomes flesh, that leads to destruction of vitality. Only 'bodily spirituality' (Sloterdijk) makes us open to the world, redeeming the subject from his abstract isolation.

At issue is 'the body, open to the world, becoming more radiant', 'the body becoming more eloquent and more expressive of the world'.[3] I increasingly have the impression that 'bodily spirituality' is awakening among a growing number of people. I observe that these people, who are freer of imposed opinions, think less controversially. Despite all their critical capacity for making distinctions, even when they say 'No,' they initially seek and signal contact and connections: the 'Yes' in the 'No' and the 'No' in the 'Yes'. Understanding becomes possible with them within the depths of the Dionysian feeling of us, of being bound together, rather than in terms of a superficial, levelling-down cosmopolitanism. Status, mask, and appearance become less important. Sensing oneself bodily also makes talk vital and creative. The person whose energy derives from the Dionysian spirit isn't dependent on wars so as to sense his body. How remote from both body and mind appear so many proclaimers of the word become flesh, how isolated with their universal message!

THE ENERGY-BASED HUMAN

The energy-based human being doesn't feel and need to force himself on and shape other people and things. He or she lives out of the exciting feeling that people and things come to him, 'involving him in the adventure of experience'.[4] He doesn't surrender himself but allows things to happen. He consents to what occurs. He knows that it is impossible to step into the same river twice (Heraclitus), keeping himself free and available. He anticipates lethargic resistance and is relaxedly alert. His relationships flourish because he doesn't hold onto people. He succeeds in much because he doesn't want to achieve anything. He doesn't strive to be an original personality. He's more concerned about understanding and relationship. And yet it is particularly in such a person that life gives characteristic expression to itself. He is attracted to things rather than being dependent, someone who devotes himself to rather than oppressing others. Whatever seeks expression is directed towards rather than against others. He experiences himself as a moon-like creature, viewing the light he throws on others as a reflection of their own. Such energy-based human beings do not blind one another but instead enjoy and thrive in the 'sunbaths' they receive. No contradiction is involved in the fact that they are more active than people who devote all their will-power to self-confirmation. With their relaxed openness, energy-based human beings attract energy.

Their words do not obstruct the flesh becoming the word, and no preconceived ideas hinder gestures.

ELEVEN

Traumatic and Erotic Patterns

I didn't intend to relate another of my dreams in this book. Mention of the first dream at the beginning wasn't planned either. It simply came to me in the night before I started writing, and since the dream changed my entire attitude towards the project I had no alternative but to recount it. The situation is similar at present. Yesterday evening I made notes as the basis for writing this chapter today. And then came a dream which seems so much more complete than what I'd previously prepared that I have to tell it. I first wondered whether I should make use of literary licence and attribute the dream to someone else, but it demonstrates a number of details that have already been mentioned. My trick would be seen through, undermining such a strategy. Anyone who writes psycho-energetically, allowing what is written to emerge out of the moment, creates an unusual mixture of the unscheduled and the planned, of what is happening now and what already existed. Now for the dream.

I was walking towards the town, along the Lindstrasse, in my birthplace Winterthur. From the other direction came a beautiful, dark haired women with intense Asiatic eyes – clad in black and around thirty-five in a wheelchair. She seemed to be in distress and looked at me in search of help. When we were alongside one another, she immediately started speaking: 'I've written to you three times and you didn't answer. I always wrote about the same thing – something that happened throughout my life from childhood onwards: about my father who went off, and my husband who left me. And now you too don't answer me. I've already tried to kill myself three times. And you don't react at all!' I was confused, made excuses, and thought of the many letters from readers, still lying unanswered on my desk. At that point the first scene broke off, but the dream continued.

Once again I am walking along the Lindstrasse, but this time away from the town. And again I see a woman in a wheelchair who looks similar and is the same age. She could be the first woman's twin. But she is moving in the same direction as me, about ten metres in front. I immediately feel a greater attraction towards her than towards the other. She turns around, stretches out her arms to me, and I walk faster. When I reach her I grasp both hands, feeling pleasurable warmth and energy. She doesn't say anything but looks at me as if ready for an adventure. Finally she asks: 'Did you hold the other's hands too?' Full of consternation I confess to myself that I had omitted to do so. I hold the second woman's hands even more tightly. She becomes ever more cheerful, laughs for joy, and gets out of the wheelchair with great ease as if that were a matter of course. We leave the wheelchair, which suddenly becomes as small as a children's seat, and walk on quickly and exuberantly.

On the right I see, with a feeling of happiness, a Greek sacred site in dazzling sunlight where in reality there is a little park. In the foreground, at the foot of a hill with a number of temples, is a spacious Greek theatre whose semi-circular stone auditorium descends to the stage. We are now close to this theatre. My companion asks me: 'Have you been here before?' I say no, and she responds by shaking her head disbelievingly. She points to the theatre, explaining: 'That is the theatre of Dionysos'. Then she indicates two free-standing pillars with doric capitals, marvellously luminous and towering to the right of the theatre. 'Those are the heliotropes'. I say to my guide: 'Let's go in!'

DREAM ANALYSIS

Even without any knowledge of the life story involved here, closer consideration throws light on the dream from within. So I'll only provide information on a single detail, allowing the dream to otherwise speak for itself. I am aware that the dream has more to tell me than is communicated here. Its essential message is, however, archetypal, and therefore also accessible to someone unaware of related aspects of my life. I'll pursue the theme of this chapter – traumatic and erotic patterns – by carrying on dreaming whilst awake. I go beyond what its symbolism signifies for my personal existence, adding aspects familiar to me from work as a therapist.

The detailed information is as follows. The Lindstrasse was the way I used to take to primary school, planted on both sides with old lime trees, and for me associated with many loving memories. On the right hand side (when leaving the town) after about two hundred metres there was a locked wrought iron gate behind which stood an old villa in a park whose huge trees prevented the gaze from penetrating further. Today, so far as I know, the park is open to the public. For me this used to be the most exciting and mysterious park imaginable. When in my late adolescence I heard Charles Trenet's chanson *Le jardin extraordinaire*, which today still casts a spell over me, I immediately thought of this park. The singer walks with the goddess Artemis, past statues, speaking owls, and murmuring springs, and participates in nocturnal balls. This mysterious park out of my childhood thus served to throw light on a highly symbolic dream image in which the miraculous became a cultural landscape.

The first two scenes in the dream take place on the same street but with me going in opposite directions. The way into the town leads to order and structure. When I take that way I cannot come together, and continue, with the woman who is an image of my own life. Our ways cross, and we leave one another without having attained accord. I am thereby frustrating my own life plan. If, however, I travel out of the town, out of the ordered into the disordered, the freely growing, I take the same direction as the second woman, who in turn depicts my unconscious existence. Establishing contact with this woman is sufficient for healing. She stands up and walks. The paralysis is over, and life open.

Moving towards nature rather than the town is not indicated in all problematic situations. There are, after all, also situations where we need, at least for the moment, identification and security within what is familiar. So what problem is involved here, making necessary taking leave of what is well known and familiar because that signifies illness? At issue is the necessary leaving behind of *traumatic patterns* embodied by the first woman in the wheelchair[1] – in other words, traces of the affect resulting from an early psychological wound. The woman's legs are paralysed, and she cannot therefore gain a foothold on the ground of reality. She doesn't stand on her own legs, and doesn't make progress naturally. That symptom of illness is the visualisation of a psychological disturbance. What wrong attitude is manifested here? Once again, clinging to the traumatic patterns. It is time for me to explain that, or rather let the dream explain it.

The woman hopes that she'll be helped as a result of talking about the trauma of being unloved. Three times she was abandoned – by her father, her husband, and 'me'; three times she attempted to commit suicide; and three times she wrote to 'me'. Three is the number that expresses dynamism. This woman's dynamism expresses itself by constantly scratching open the old wounds of being unloved. In the process she makes demands, and shows no understanding for delays in 'my' dealing with correspondence. Time and again she wants to talk about her suffering, describe her bad father in all details, and probe her villainous husband's unpleasantness so as to rid herself of any guilt feelings about separation from him. Her trick – utilising endless analysis so as to avoid entering life and going beyond the trauma – does not work. She cultivates resistance by lavishing care and attention on the wound of being unloved, which demands much time and money. So that's what my life looks like when I remain caught up in traumatic patterns.

What a corrosive and undermining influence is exerted by masochistically nurtured bad memories! They signify an absolutely self-destructive, suicidal course. Traumatic patterns lead to psychological destruction as Franz Kafka's fate demonstrates. Human beings are highly sensitive auto-suggestive systems. We determine our fate by resuscitation of such old memories, unbalancing our lives. We also carry on rummaging around in old wounds when we already know everything possible about them, thereby creating new wounds until our entire existence entails suffering and burning pain is our only feeling. We thus hypnotise ourselves with the message: 'Everything is as it always was'. Brooding over old wounds involves dwelling on the wound of being unloved. That can only heal if we leave it in peace. That is a matter of healing, not of repression.

A woman recently told me that when she was sticking photos into an album, she suddenly felt sharp heart pains and had to lie down. She then became aware that these family photos dated back to the time when her husband had a severe heart attack. She had thus unconsciously hypnotised herself and identified with her husband, suffering anew what was long past. Making people aware of such auto-hypnotic processes is healing since it furthers dissociation from triggering a traumatic memory and from the compulsion to return for the thousandth time to an old story of suffering. *Being unable to forget* causes suffering within traumatic patterns. Only composure in the face of old psychological wounds gradually brings about healing forgetfulness of emotions even if the facts have not been erased from memory.

TRAUMATIC PATTERNS IN CHRISTIANITY

In Christianity (and particularly in the Western Church) a terrible intensification of traumatic patterns within individuals occurred and still occurs as a result of the collective memory of Jesus's death. It is not the pains of growth that the Man of Sorrows suffers in artistic depictions. Resurrection and transformation are seldom indicated. For two thousand years now he has bled from his five wounds: a hypnotic image that has intensified, if not created, traumatic patterns in innumerable people. Jesus and many saints appear as defenceless victims. Trust in the patterns of growth is seldom apparent in the Christian art of the Western Church. In the Eastern Church, however, the interrelationship between death and transformation becomes more frequently apparent. On Russian icons, for instance, the blood drips from the crucified Christ's right side down onto Adam's skull at the foot of the cross so as to include the first man (and humanity per se) in renewed life. Traditional Christianity of course sees that as being in the next world rather than this.

The traumatic pattern pursued by the first woman in the dream also leads into other psychological areas of misery. We must visit those too so as to become free for the encounter with the second woman and the erotic pattern she pursues.

From the many possible symptoms I select three which allow the traumatic pattern of inability to forget to become clearly apparent.

A life in a wheelchair as a psychological image of people who cut themselves off from the lower half of their body is expressed in stomach pains as well as in reduced sexuality and eroticism. Links between stomach pains and psychological separation from body and world are to be found in autobiographical testimony by two celebrated philosophers as well as in textbooks devoted to psychosomatics. For the Christian gnostic philosopher Plotinus (third century AD), 'being in the body' and 'being in the world' entailed banishment and alienation. Like St. Paul, he yearned for liberation from 'the body of this death', and suffered – as he himself reported – from absolutely unbearable stomach pains. He was happy about that because he saw those pains as a sign that he was gradually separating himself from the material world. His diagnosis is accurate. Psychologically derived stomach pains are symptoms of the withdrawal of life-energy from the body. Why are pains localised in the stomach? Probably for two reasons. Firstly, the stomach is a place of transmutation where material nourishment from the outer world becomes bodily being. That is why the stomach is particularly susceptible to our resistance to the physical and material. Secondly, it is situated in the middle of the body. Rejection of the entire body is centred there. For its part the lower half of the body – and thus the sexual sphere – is affected by hostility to the body up to the point of complete numbing and lack of sensitivity. The stomach is still capable of suffering when the sexual sphere has already lost capacity for sensation. It is as if rejection of the fleshly mounts within the body from below upwards as a psychological paralysis.

We can be happy about stomach pains for contrary reasons to Plotinus. They indicate that we haven't as yet completely separated ourselves from this world, and that the body is still alive, albeit only in terms of its pain. By welcoming psychologically caused stomach pains as a messenger of the living body, which revolts against ominously rising paralysis, we move from the traumatic to the erotic pattern.

Sixteen hundred years later, Nietzsche, the other suffering philosopher, remarked on the same connection between separation from the body and stomach pains, but from a different perspective. He wrote that he got stomach pains every time he thought of God. He suffered from stomach pains very often, so he must have thought of God a great deal. Nietzsche comprehended his suffering as a sign that he was not in his body when he devoted attention to this 'thought God'. 'Thinking that is . . . nausea for the stomach. Conjecturing such a thing (that is, a reality behind the thought God) is truly a churning sickness'[2]. Throughout his life Nietzsche remained someone tormented by this God, which his experiences with Christianity led him to view as being separated from body and world. Nietzsche's persistent reflection on God resulted in constant re-infection of the emotional wound of not being physically loved and not loving his physical body: a Christian fate, yet in its consciousness also a sign of the possibility of liberation.

IN SEARCH OF THE BODY

Anyone who is not in their body seeks incessantly without knowing what he seeks. He restlessly wanders the world in search of that unknown god, the body. Wilhelm Busch's words apply here: 'I'm here in any case / but pleasure is always in another place'. He thinks happiness is to be found in another country or with another partner. But scarcely has he reached somewhere new or found another partner than he is once again seized by intense unrest. He is the wanderer of whom Schubert's song of the same name says: 'Happiness is where you are absent'. He restlessly scratches at the wound of his loneliness, etching the traumatic pattern deeper into his life. If only he could sing his 'life-melody' (Alfred Adler) differently – 'Happiness is where you are completely present' – he would be pursuing eroticism. He would no longer succumb to the mistake of being 'here in any case'. As long as 'another place' is always more beautiful for him, his body is in exile and he is not really 'here'.

'Being in the body' and 'living in the moment' are psychological synonyms. A man in a feverish delirium constantly asked: 'Is it yesterday or tomorrow?' That question contains the diagnosis of his life to date. He had never lived in the reality of the present moment, but often in yesterday – in yearningly tormenting memories of what was past, that is, in the traumatic pattern – and often in tomorrow, with illusions of a future that should 'bring' everything denied in the present, i.e. also in the same traumatic pattern. He rarely pursued the pleasurable trail of life bursting with energy in the present moment, even in banal activities. He grimly went jogging but didn't know how to stroll. The body that had become sad thus became ill. When he was convalescing from a serious illness, the man gradually learnt to move with today. 'If we say "Yes" to a single moment, we have affirmed all existence rather than just ourselves' (Nietzsche). Bodily being in the present moment is always a 'being in the world' and a *'being in relationship'*. A person present in his body experiences himself as nothing but relationship. He is the *erotic pattern*. Conversely, someone who exiles himself to the past and future is absolutely cut off from relationship since he is fixated on the wound of being unloved. His life follows the traumatic trail.

For such a person the ego becomes an overvalued idea. He doesn't allow things to take their course and just happen, so he experiences his ego in the grandiose pose of withdrawal from the world. The overvaluation of the ego in Western thinking is to be explained in terms of the isolating traumatic pattern. Anyone who doesn't allow his ego to expand and flourish in its relationship to the world, miscomprehending the wound of non-relationship as one of life's particularly profound works of art, replaces uniting activity by the uncommitted self.

Finally there are *traumatising partnerships*. I've written at length about that in *How to Say No to The One You Love* and *Farewell to Self-Destruction*. Here I'd like to consider a further aspect of that theme, namely the *energy process within polar consciousness* (see chapter 4, p.30, the third experience of energy). Every relationship is polar because it is identical with the complementary pole's area of tension. The attraction that two people feel for one another is further intensified by conciousness of the polarities they embody as a couple. In both, polarities are mobilised that without this partnership would be mere possibilities and unlived life. Tension, excitement, and eroticism thus come into being. Self-centred people, on the other hand, who remain caught up in painful memories of their old wounds, are excluded from access to the polar game of a relationship. Their partnerships are boring. An unpleasant lack of tension chains them together. With what are they concerned in this desert for two? With jointly poking around in the wound of their being unloved – and their lovelessness. They find fault with themselves and others, and drag up ancient tales from their marriage: 'Even long ago you were so . . . ' . Time and again they succumb to compulsive retelling of long-exhausted conversations about their relationship. Pleasurable polarity is replaced by hostile polarisation. Disunited, they are simultaneously pursuing the traumatic trail.

If at the start of their partnership they experienced polar attraction and pleasure, the question arises: how did their polar feeling come to break down? In what way did the attraction of love turn into rejective hostility? Through long established auto-suggestion which they forgot for a while during the first flush of love but now resuscitate. In its most extreme form this auto-suggestion states: 'You're against me in all of your thoughts and deeds'. After the ecstatic opening to the other and thereby to the world during the initial period, the old traumatic closing to everything re-establishes itself. We no longer experience ourselves dynamically in the vibration of two poles but instead as opposites statically confronting one another. The early trauma – the wound of being unloved – breaks out again: I am rejected, abandoned, isolated, unloved. What alternative do two people together, following the traumatic trail, have but to excoriate each other's old wounds, causing new injuries?

Thus far the first woman in my dream has brought us. Either we go astray in an auto-hypnotic hall of mirrors where our wounds multiply themselves, or something completely new happens. That is the case in the dream.

I'm going in the same direction as the second woman. Polarity signifies relatedness, entailing adhering to the shared excitement of life and going still further along the same way. I take the hands stretched out to me. This bodily contact brings a pleasurable increase of strength. Involvement in contact awakens a connection. Our bodies tingle like electricity. Radiant energy trickles through us. You glow. We don't speak. In this moment words would be counter-productive, and we would again become objects, opposed to one another, isolated, and unloved in the traumatic pattern. *Everything new is speechless.* Anyone who talks too much now falls away into old patterns. We maintain the tension of silence. Now our bodies are gently murmuring. Life whispers. A chortle, a smile, a foolish remark, a mischievous question: 'Did you hold the other's hands too?' This amusing question with its playful jealousy leads into the depths. That is what is at issue: taking one another's hands, and dissolution of the thinking ego in the actions of love. I hold more firmly the hands of this woman who has become illumined as if to confirm the fresh insight. Energy intensifies. What is entrenched becomes light and flexible. This is the hour of joyousness. The woman gets up out of the wheelchair. Stimulation of the energy of love within the woman leads her to remember the capacity to move. The reality of the wheelchair – it is a child's seat – reveals itself in the light of our relationship. Isolation established itself in early childhood and persisted for many years. But now, thanks to an essential relationship, we awaken in the real world. We quickly abandon the child's chair, and continue cheerfully along our way, along the erotic trail.

ENABLING ORDER AND STRUCTURE

It has become light. The world shines like our eyes. A Greek cult area gleams within the realm of the self. Out of physical contact the world becomes a resplendent embodiment of culture. The Apollonian is born out of the Dionysian. The light comes from within. It shines *out of* the darkness, and not *into* the darkness as in the Gospel according to St. John. At the foot of the hill thrown up by nature and humanly completed with temples, there lies the theatre of Dionysos – both in the dream and at Athens. In the dream, the theatre and the Acropolis are linked in a single sacred site. In Athens the two were divided by a much-used road until recently. Melina Mercouri, the Greek Minister of Culture, then united the two sites in a single archaeological zone. Cultural achievements really do have to be re-united with their Dionysian origins – as with the Acropolis and the theatre of Dionysos in Athens. Dionysos is after all, as previously mentioned, ordering rhythm and self-structuring pulsation, as is shown in the history of Greek tragedy developing out of the cult of Dionysos. Psycho-energetics, which lives out of the Dionysian spirit, doesn't entail regression into undifferentiated emotionality, world renouncing ecstasy, and rapture, but rather makes possible a vital order and structure by way of affirmation of the erotic pattern, which doesn't exclude what is dark, chaotic, and destructive. Love also embraces death as the dark side of life. The pleasure principle remains nothing but an ardent wish if it doesn't expand into the energy principle, which also affirms the drive towards chaos and death, connecting it with the overall impulse towards life.

Two tall, free-standing pillars rise into the sky to the right of the temple of Dionysos. Their golden radiance dominates my memory of the site. My guide calls them 'heliotropes', directly from the Greek: 'turning to the sun', like sunflowers ('tournesol' in French and 'girasole' in Italian) which do the same as the heliotrope, a species of plant that grows in all warm countries. Turning towards the sun and the light, thereby seeking the radiance of the world and the other, assimilating and reflecting this in moon-like fashion rather than being narcissistically preoccupied with one's own light, is the attitude of the energy-based human being I have described. That takes place of its own accord within opening up to the convalescent woman in the dream. Pursuing the trail of greatest feeling doesn't signify a retreat into one's own world of feelings, but rather a striving for expression, devotion, and gesture. The lover doesn't ask who is loving. He merely knows that love is at work. In Japanese the little sentence 'I love you' is simply expressed with the verb's infinitive, with the activity 'to love'. If the 'I' places itself at the beginning, loving remains incomplete. The 'compulsion towards identity' (Michael Foucault) diminishes the devotion. Loving is exclusively relationship. Pillars remain turned towards the sun throughout the day. They are 'heliotropes', eternally dedicated to the light thanks to their roundness.

The depressed collapse inwardly whereas lovers stand up straight. The two pillars symbolise how the woman and I attain our rightful magnitude within the splendour of love which furthers growth. I assume that these pillars are dedicated to Apollo. Life grows out of the Dionysian contact of love to become an Apollonian work of art. Each of the pillars stands on its own. And yet the essence of both lies in the 'between' (Martin Buber), in the space between the two. The lover is the relationship to the beloved. If we stand between two pillars or two tree-trunks, attentively sensing what is happening, we observe that their being exists in the empty space between them, in the fluctuating energy's area of tension.

Someone who broods is a person without initiative. An alertly receptive person, on the other hand, who apparently lethargically holds back, blinking at the sun and attracting things to himself by way of expectant delight, takes the initiative at the right moment. The time is ripe for entering the 'extraordinary garden', the zone of the miraculous. At the end of the dream the dreamer says: 'Let's go in'. In the East I've observed people sitting without moving for hours, and then suddenly, following a signal imperceptible to me, getting up and setting to work with great speed and concentration.

Didn't I too enter the realm of the miraculous by discarding my original plan for this chapter, holding onto the guideline provided by the dream, and returning step by step to the light out of the 'entrails of the unconscious'? By unfolding the theme of the traumatic and erotic patterns with Dionysian turbulence rather than with cool Apollonian detachment? Writing a psychology book by following where the energy takes you is at any rate a remarkable business, a process involving one's own emotional expressiveness and transformation. The spectator discovers to his astonishment that he is nothing but a performer. He vanishes from the audience and finds himself on stage, which is suddenly everything. This 'leap onto the stage', which I described in 1980[4], is an awakening in the world.

BREATHING

Finally, I would like to explain a possibility of determining at any moment whether we are on the traumatic or the erotic trail. This derives from the *psycho-energetics of breathing*. The flow of breathing involves two directions: breathing out into the external world, and breathing in into the inner self. A healthy person pulsates in this dual movement of breathing between the outer world and himself. If he breathes out, his interest spontaneously goes outwards and his attention is directed towards 'the world'. When he breathes in, interest spontaneously goes inwards and the objective is 'the self'. The fundamental pulsation of our 'being in the world' is thus demonstrated in breathing. In the rhythm of giving and taking, self-abandonment and differentiation, we maintain a balance within this our flow. If we are very attentive during a tranquil moment, we notice that when breathing out – particularly just before the transition to breathing in – the periphery of our body (and especially the organs of contact: hands, feet, eyes, and sexual organs) become more charged and sensitive, tingling or vibrating slightly. When we are breathing in – above all just before the transition to breathing out – the stomach as the centre of the body charges itself with energy. The focus of energy follows the rhythm of breathing in and out by moving outwards towards the periphery of the body and then inwards to its centre.

The healthy person's experiencing flows in unconscious attunement with the dual movement of his breathing. If he breathes in, he is spontaneously more strongly concentrated inwardly, and when he breathes out he expands outwardly to a greater extent. That is demonstrated in practical terms by the fact that he begins some physical activity by exhaling, and always first does so if some special effort is involved. He breathes out during any intensive sporting activity such as the long jump or high jump. Even if he only gets up from the table, he does so while exhaling. That occurs of its own accord and is not some special technique. When he exhales he moves into the world, and when he inhales he withdraws. He alternately experiences himself within achievement whilst exhaling and within the gathering of energy when inhaling. His inner eye moves outwardly whilst exhaling and inwardly whilst inhaling. For such a person the centrifugal and centripetal movement of energy involves an undivided and unified experience.

Among people with traumas of abandonment, who thus suffer from the wound of being unloved, there occurs a *division between the biological process and the subjective experience*. They experience the centrifugal movement of breath (that is, exhalation) with a centripetal movement of the emotions, and vice versa. What does that entail?

I have observed that many clients almost imperceptibly withdraw into themselves when exhaling, slightly tensing their muscles as if under invisible pressure, whilst during inhalation they relax slightly and open up. Such contradictory behaviour seemed very strange and started to interest me. Why when they breathe out do they behave as if they were being pumped out under external pressure? And why do they seem able to face the outer world more relaxedly when breathing in? These subtle contradictions demand sensitive attentiveness from the observer. They provide very precise and illuminating information about a person's basic energy problems because they reflect his or her fundamental rhythmic structure.

This split mainly expresses itself in exhalation among people who feel oppressive pressure (see chapter 9) instead of a pleasurable lust for life. They don't release themselves into the world with exhalation. They hold anxiously onto their ego rather than experiencing their potency in communication of the self and devotion. Their energy cannot thereby flow unhindered outwardly, so they feel a lack of pleasure and power, and the outer world as correspondingly overwhelming. It is particularly at the moment of exhalation where an unprotected letting go would be appropriate that they concentrate desperately on themselves, seeking protection. When breathing out and expressing himself, a stutterer, for instance, seemed always to be suffering from some invisible external pressure, which obstructed what he wanted to say. His stuttering was a particularly clear-cut sign of ambivalence in self-expression. Other indications may often be less conspicuous but are equally definite. For instance, a woman told me that she experienced depression as compression in her breast. I then asked her to pay attention to what happened during inhalation and exhalation to her compressed, choked breast. After a number of breaths she said that the pressure was greater when she breathed out. Her fear of love was thus most tormenting during the bodily movement of letting go.

Heavy smokers who inhale are also afraid of giving themselves. They greedily draw the smoke inside themselves as if they could never get enough mother's milk. Both inhalation and exhalation present problems, inhibiting the capacity to give themselves. Their relationships are either over-structured and concerned with protection against the unpredictable, or their partnerships involve brief compulsive phases between longer periods of non-communication.

INTEGRATING BIOLOGICAL PROCESS AND PSYCHOLOGICAL EXPERIENCE

When our self-experiencing accords with our breathing, we don't need to pay any further attention to inhalation and exhalation. Thinking about it would make us feel insecure and disturb our natural rhythm. But someone suffering from a trauma, who becomes aware of the reversed biological rhythm in breathing in and out (and thereby of the psychological rhythm of yielding and obstructing), gradually experiences, without any special effort, a change thanks to this fresh consciousness of the misguided association of exhalation with self-preservation and inhalation with establishment of relationships. He or she can make this process easier by inwardly saying the words 'let go' or 'world' when exhaling, and 'take in' or 'self' when inhaling. The person concerned thus finds composure in mounting correspondence between the biological process and the psychological experience. He or she can ultimately forget about paying attention in this way to breathing in and out since the flow of breath has become a holistic biological and psychological occurrence. Both inhalation and exhalation then only involve the unobstructed flow of breath and life-energy. Self and world are relativised in this new composure, and distinctions are blurred when they are experienced as merely the two phases within the single pulsation.

As long as we endow breathing in and out with contrary psychological messages, we are on the traumatic trail. If, however, body and psyche come together in a single stream of lived experience, we are linked with everything alive and are pursuing the erotic pattern.

TWELVE

Participation in the Suffering of the Unloved Child

The wound of being unloved is speechless. It has no words for healing itself. The unloved may tell many stories about how they were rejected, emotionally abandoned, and misunderstood, but these always refer to times of life when they could already express their suffering in words. The speechless period of the first months of life is not given verbal expression even at a later stage. If people do nevertheless later indulge in conjecture about that time, they often seem to be less touched by their own words than the subject matter would lead one to assume, or they feel they're saying something wrong, even if what's said is confirmed by other testimony. Language was not a means of expression with which they could have made known their former suffering. It is thus equally unsuited for later communication of early and still speechless suffering. The unloved will never be able to express in words what happened to them as embryos and babies.

The trauma of being unloved goes back to the speechless time before and after birth. Conversations within therapy about later experiences of being unloved often serve as alibis distracting from the root cause – the still speechless wound of being unloved. For lack of other possibilities people talk about something that cannot be approached and grasped by way of words. The speechless root cause must first be able to give expression to itself, and then the words that register later experiences of being unloved would be grounded and meaningful. As it is they are in a state of limbo. This apparently insoluble dilemma often leads to endless analysis or to an embittered breaking off of analysis before the longed for breakthrough has been achieved.

Is that dilemma really insoluble? Can't the small child, lacking command over words, finally express itself in some appropriate wordless fashion as an adult years or decades later? Or must analysis ultimately remain a strategy for avoiding the roots of suffering, for gaining such ego-strength that one is not overwhelmed by profound inner pain, and for stoically putting up with life? I attempt to answer those questions in this chapter.

MISSING THE POINT

The wound of being unloved is not just the outcome of individual events in the life of a child, as when the parents were once away for a moment just when the crying child awoke from a nightmare. Need of an explanation often leads the adult unloved to construct interconnections that don't touch the heart of his or her condition. The fact that such explanations only spark off minor emotional reactions among the people concerned demonstrates that they miss the point. They belong in the sphere of the previously mentioned forms of alibi analysis. The situation is different when several specific events where the child felt left in the lurch point to a fundamental attitude of the mother, father, or both towards their offspring. It is highly probable that this attitude already existed during the speechless initial phase of life. This exerts a devastating impact on the embryo and the new-born child during the most impressionable age. The destructive parental attitude perhaps involved an absence or an excess of feeling, concealing lack of real relatedness to this particular child, or ongoing negative aggression, or, in general terms, some personality defect. A baby is a feeling being which needs attention and love for its development, not a creature consisting of nothing but reflexes and instincts.

In some cases it is difficult, even impossible, to establish connections between the wound of being unloved and the most important people in someone's life. Sometimes, albeit rarely, that wound seems to originate largely or even exclusively in the personality of those who feel unloved, and to a lesser extent, or even not at all, in crucial figures from that early stage. I know of the tragic fates of people who

lived and died almost in isolation where lack of parental love was not the cause. The determining dynamics of
predisposition shouldn't be underestimated. Parents should
know that children can suffer the fate of feeling unloved
despite the fact that they obviously were sufficiently loved.
But even parents who later admit to a great lack of love
for their children shouldn't destroy themselves with useless
guilt feelings. They did what was possible in terms of their
own life story. What is at stake now is to rescue the child
that they themselves are from itself being unloved. Then
they will spread love rather than lovelessness. The feeling
of being unloved almost always arises out of a mixture of
external influences and personal disposition. In this book I
am primarily concerned with the former since psychotherapy
must start there.

The necessary mention of serious genetic factors, which can
help cause a person's isolation, shouldn't, however, lead to
any playing down of the tragic impact of a real lack of love
for a small child. In most people we can trace an important
element in the feeling of being unloved back to the childhood
situation. That is most clearly apparent in adults who were in
children's homes and suffered from hospitalism – that is, from
psychological forms of lack of bodily closeness and attention
during their upbringing. A baby in such a home misses
emotional exchange and consolatory soothing. It must wait
for meals, and so on. Above all it lacks inner closeness to the
mother, and thus security. Hospitalism (the term was coined
by René Spitz) among children from such homes has been
closely observed and described over the past two decades.
We can assume that little children suffer similarly in the
seclusion of their families, but there the forms of emotional
deprivation are for the most part more subtle and more difficult to penetrate.

How do small children express a sense of abandonment?
Through psycho-motor restlessness linked with screaming,
which particularly intensifies before meals to the point
of great excitement. Sleep and intake of nourishment are
frequently also disturbed. Profound abandonment is apparent in the facial expression: down-turned corners of the
mouth, deep folds in the nose, knitted eyebrows, and tense
rather than relaxed features. 'If you pick up one of these

babies crying so desperately, it can often calm down surprisingly even though still without its bottle'. It is 'human contact that satisfies and calms'.[1]

What happens if abandonment becomes a lasting state? The small child's reactions of protest diminish. Auto-erotic activities increase, replacing the mother's attention. Stereotyped forms of movement develop in place of the free motor activity of a loved child. 'The child that is deprived of emotional attention . . . directs aggression against itself'[2] because it lacks the confidence for discovering its environment by way of grasping and grabbing. Erik Erikson attributes lack of primal confidence among adults to early abandonment of the small child.

We shouldn't shrink from talking about a lack of *love* as the cause of all symptoms of abandonment. A human science that shies away from the most human words suffers from a linguistic fear of contact. That is why I called this book *The Wound of the Unloved* rather than *The Wound of the Abandoned*. There are children who are outwardly never abandoned, and may often be held and carried, but are never really loved. This lack of love, which is often just a scarcely perceptible feeling, can always be demonstrated on closer observation by way of more subtle indications in the parents' behaviour. This is, however, above all a reality intensively felt by the child.

CLIENT-INITIATED THERAPIST

I'd now like to provide a therapeutic impulse showing how the still wordless small child – whose self-expression remains limited because of lack of love – can nevertheless find liberating features in the 'playroom' of the place of therapy. Two preliminary remarks are necessary. It would be wrong to decide on the basis of the following description that I constantly or predominantly work 'non-verbally'. There are analyses where that is never the case – at least not in this obvious and exclusive way. The way the therapist proceeds depends on the client, not vice versa. Profound, overwhelming experiences cannot be pre-planned and multiplied. A single one can be sufficient if it then provides fresh orientation for everyday existence through verbal depiction of what happened. One experience can offer a sense of the erotic pattern. Love, reverence, and sobriety are also requisite in the client's attitude to such events. Seeking such experiences time and again would mean succumbing to the compulsive repetitiveness of addiction and rapid loss of the energy pattern just found. The wound of being unloved would open up again and again. This addiction would also be a surrogate for love.

Secondly, such events are among the most intimate and personal a human being can experience. He or she here completely experiences his or her origins and very self. For that very reason it wouldn't be acceptable for the author of a book to reveal to anonymous readers the innermost life of someone who entrusted himself to the analyst. Even when there is no danger of this client's identity being recognised, his first bringing to the light of hitherto obscured and hidden events within his life story should not be subjected to the spotlight of publicity, lacking the warmth of an affectionate glance. Another circumstance nonetheless makes it possible to write about such experiences. The basic elements within such primal events, which constitute the most inward and personal aspects of an individual, are at the same time the most general, the most human, and the most profoundly familiar to everyone: archetypal primal gestures in human development. Once again it becomes apparent here that 'individuation' entails 'participation': involvement in what is entailed in being fully human. It is above all when I have the feeling of acting most individually and personally that I am united by way of a primal human gesture with all human beings. Anyone who falls in love for the first time has the impression of experiencing something absolutely new, even if millions of people have previously experienced this. In the example I'll now present, I have several people in mind simultaneously. I'll concentrate on what is common to them all, only mentioning particular aspects when they don't involve anything intimate. In order to make this easier to read I have summarised what these people share in a single fictional character.

After a fairly prolonged period of cautiously feeling his way within the analytical conversation, this man gradually developed trust. This new attitude was, however, still easily upset. If I am slightly late or inattentive, or refer to 'social reality', he takes that as a withdrawal of love and reason for renewed distrust. He's on the lookout: should he venture out, or must he attack? It often happens that I notice what feeling would like to be given expression in him, freely vibrating. I thus become a sounding-board for a timid, still unconscious emotion in the person opposite me. I realise, for instance, that I am vibrating with his anger, demonstrating solidarity with his rage at a time when he still believes himself to simply lack any energy or desire, or feels a completely different emotion such as sadness. His secretly throbbing anger is already resounding in me without restriction and he is ever more trustingly linked with me, so that I can now – almost wordlessly and primarily through emotional emanation – initiate liberation of his emotion. That now also attains resonance and expression within him, and his anger breaks through with unrestrained violence. He remains within this anger until finally achieving relaxation and release. A frozen gesture has become fluid, awakening an abundance of insights, new dream motifs, and existential impulses. I have given a detailed description of what is involved in this energy process of resonance in *Farewell to Self-Destruction*.[3]

FINDING THE ROOT CAUSE

Such emotionally powerful moments remain rare in this man's therapy. Immobilisation, distrust, and despair time and again gain the upper hand. Within his existence there still seems to be something older and more fundamental than anger, awaiting the gesture of resolution. This blocks the life that flows in moments of emotional attunement. We both sense that the decisive factor still remains undecided.

One day I see something new which I had never previously observed even though it was always there. In the man sitting opposite me, now starting to cry out of desperation over his unhappy relationships, I suddenly perceive the baby his mother didn't love properly. My perception is partly based on external signs: the helplessness and despair in his strangulated screams, the unco-ordinated and cramped movements of arms and legs, the impotent weakness displayed in sudden withdrawal within himself – all signs of complete dependence. Intuition suddenly leads me to ask whether he would like to lie down – which he immediately does without saying a word. He doesn't say any more and looks fixedly ahead as if wanting to make sure of not losing track of what has just happened. The strangulated sobs intensify to become penetrating screams expressing complete abandonment. He attempts to sit up with his hands opening and closing, nervously twitching here and there. He then abruptly falls back into total powerlessness. That process is repeated several times. His limbs wriggle, thrash around, and writhe in persistent spasms. The screams become ever more desperate.

I allow myself to be moved by this baby's efforts at getting its mother at long last to take him in her arms, holding, carrying, and rocking him. I can't just sit there. I have to participate in the child's painful endeavours. I watch him steadfastly while he still gazes into emptiness with his eyes wide open.

If he tries to sit up, the head is the first thing to fall back. The tension in his weak back and neck is terrible to see. I say softly that he should lay his hands on top of one another on the stomach and breathe deeply. Time and again he lifts himself in a desperate silent cry for his mother, but the contact between hands and stomach slowly makes him somewhat calmer. It's as if he's starting to give himself security and attention. If his hands again flail nervously over the stomach, I repeat that he should place them there somewhat more firmly. His breathing now gets deeper of its own accord. The spasmodic twitching gradually declines and he relaxes. The energy flows in longer, slower waves. A feeling of inner closeness and agreeable freshness spreads. The man is gently crying to himself. His face looks happily relaxed. I turn away from him, let him lie for a while, and then suggest he should get up and sit opposite me.

A woman told me after such an experience that her back pains had vanished and a man that the tension in his neck was no longer there. Sometimes I have the feeling that the person sitting in front of me is now really seeing me for the first time. A woman herself said: 'I'm seeing you for the first time'. That's not surprising. The therapist's sympathy makes it possible for the hitherto incomplete and frozen gesture, suffering from lack of love, to take its natural course from screaming for the mother by way of security with the mother to a partner-like relationship. A child whose development is accompanied by the warm gaze of someone closely related can return that. It possesses the power of vital looking, which in the adult becomes the power of entering into a relationship.

WHO IS THE 'PARENT-PERSON'?

But who really was the 'mother', the 'father', or, in general terms, the 'parent-person' in what happened? Did I take on the role of mother? To a certain extent the answer to this question is Yes since from me there came 'the gleam in the mother's eye' (Winnicott) or, better still, the warmth and vitality in the parent-person's gaze, the 'empathy' (Kohut), the alert and devoted participation, the being present for the child. And yet I wasn't a baby's parent-person. I didn't pick up, hold, feed, carry, or rock this man. Such behaviour on my part might perhaps have consoled him but wouldn't have helped – not to mention the strength that would have been necessary. As an adult he has fully formed back muscles allowing him to sit up, a strong neck for holding his head, and autonomous possibilities of standing up, walking, feeding himself, and taking what he needs for life. So he doesn't need a mother or father as a baby does. Such a parent-person could no longer exist for him. Krishnamurti once said after a severe spiritual crisis when he certainly felt abandoned and unloved: 'There isn't any mother'. And that very insight was the source of his healing. For the man I've talked about my sympathetic look was nothing more than a minor impetus, which always intervened like an electrical impulse when his contact with the archetypal gesture of a baby seeking and finding its mother became uncertain.

A doctor dreamt he was suffering from the 'morbus stop' disease. Electrical current was lacking in a chain of people (including himself) holding each other's hands. They were plugged into the mains but the extension lead wasn't long enough to link up the human chain with the electricity. The feeling of: 'It doesn't reach. I never reach far enough' is a basic feeling within being unloved, putting a brake on and blocking every relationship. If someone – perhaps the therapist – who establishes contact is now there, fresh experience develops:

'Le courant passe', 'the current flows', and, figuratively, love fluctuates. The 'stop disease' is healed, but only definitely when we can ourselves establish contact with other people.

Anyone who can at long last live out early suffering in the sympathetic presence of another person goes further than his or her suffering. He or she discovers their power. Now they can give themselves what their mother or father withheld: emotional attention, warmth, dependability, and satisfaction of basic needs.

Only suffering that has got stuck is destructive. Suffering that has been freed so as to be given full expression is creative. Human beings are essentially concerned with relationships, and for that liberation they need another person to whom they risk showing themselves. Such presentation of the self should not be confused with exhibitionism. The genuineness and inwardness within the event described, and the sparingly expressive seriousness which only permits necessary gestures, offer unmistakable testimony to an essential occurrence leading to change. The therapist's intuition grasps and selects the most charged moment for such an experience. If you set that in motion too soon, there's a danger of an artificial performance. Therapy would then become cheap showmanship, and also tragically block this channel of healing. The unloved incline particularly often towards 'hysterical', importunate gestures because they are particularly ambitious without, however, believing in fulfilment of their ambitions, and also because people leave 'freaks' in peace. A woman told me that you handle with kid gloves someone who reacts to external demands by putting on a great show. This tendency towards theatricality usually disappears, however, when the therapist devotes unreservedly warm and alert attention to the expressions of early suffering.

Heidi Widmer, the artist I've previously mentioned, has recently painted several pictures where two small human figures are moving behind one another through a huge labyrinth of nets. The second figure sometimes reveals traces of wings. It offers protection to the first figure by following behind, preserving a certain distance which arouses in the spectator (dependent on individual mood) a feeling of freedom or loneliness. The therapist is not a leader either, going before. He leads by following, as a woman recently wrote to me.[4]

LOOKING FOR HEALING

In everyone's life there are spheres where no one has as yet followed. These are the isolated zones of non-love where his or her foot gets stuck. The person concerned ossifies in an eternally unresolved gesture, like the inhabitants of Pompeii who were suddenly turned to stone when enveloped by lava from the erupting Vesuvius. But if someone is there behind you and keeps going, the mummified foot defies all expectations by coming to life again, and once more there is a way forward. Only that particular person knows the way of healing and salvation. Even if he should want to, the 'one who walks behind' cannot lead the way. After all there is no pre-established objective, only the erotic pattern, the trail of the strongest feeling. This trail is mindfulness at every moment – the foot that walks because it walks.

The spell governing zones of earlier petrification has now been broken. Loneliness becomes freedom because someone is walking behind. Areas contaminated by an earlier lack of love become accessible. Even if the therapist is no longer there, the experience remains. 'Things are alright. I'm going ahead. I now know what I need for life'. The trail we follow is that of sensing at every moment.

PART FOUR

Liberating

THIRTEEN

Mental Massage
or the Purring Cat

What is our situation when outer pressure has changed into inner impulse, the traumatic into the erotic pattern, and childhood injuries and insults into an unrestricted flow of emotion? Who is the human being whose vital potential has been liberated? Does he or she feel loved unquestioningly and secure in the world? Is the love of self and the other unbroken? Has the wound of being unloved miraculously vanished? Does that therefore entail a neurotic rather than an existential problem? I'll be pursuing these and similar questions in the last part of this book.

As a preliminary, I invite the reader to participate in a practical experience which unmistakably shows that our organism possesses an unimaginably great potential for self-healing. All we need do so as to bring about stimulation of that potential is to devote relaxed, benevolent attention to what occurs of its own accord if we don't interfere. It isn't love, but fear of love, that requires therapy. Love breaks spontaneously into our lives as soon as resistance vanishes. That is true of both love of another and self-love. This chapter is concerned with the unfolding of self-love through devoting impartial attention to autonomous processes in one's own body. The conscious attention we devote to ourselves doesn't involve auto-suggestion. I don't talk myself into believing that my body is radiantly healthy. Instead I allow the body to give expression to itself, and am even ready to listen to painful messages. I'm not suggesting some violent way involving sudden discharge, like diarrhoea or emotional eruptions. This is an inward, intimate way of gaining consciousness whereby unhealthy cramps and tensions dissolve themselves

once we take account of them. If people who were unloved at
an early age lavish on themselves the warm attention they
previously lacked, they experience themselves anew as being
loved. Ultimately it is the love we give ourselves within the
flow of mindful living that heals us of early deprivation, not
the love offered by someone else.

THE BENEFITS OF MENTAL MASSAGE

Mental massage serves as a way of practising attentiveness
to the body. We 'massage' ourselves in the mind. That
brings about relaxation and well-being like a good body
massage whose secret partly entails the person being treated
entering into and merging with the masseur's movements.
Every effective body massage is thus also an involuntary
mental massage. There is no recuperation and recovery
without inner attunement to what the masseur or masseuse
is doing with our body. Aim-oriented ego-consciousness is
thus excluded. In mental massage, attentiveness, moving
over and through the body, operates in place of the masseur.
The experience gained sounds banal: 'I sense what happens
in my body of its own accord.' The unloved are of the
opinion that effort and discipline are necessary for the
gaining of well-being. That's why sensitivity to what's
simply taking place is new and liberating for them. Five
influences contributed towards my development of mental
massage. Firstly, autogenous training where attention is also
devoted to the body but through auto-suggestion which is
not used in mental massage. Neither is the emphasis on a
specific succession of exercises. Secondly, Gerda Boyesen's
massage technique in biodynamics whose objective is, so
to speak, the melting down and digestion of psychological
disturbances within the body. Boyesen uses a stethoscope to
listen to the intestinal sounds which spontaneously develop
in the course of a massage, thereby ascertaining its effectiveness in specific parts of the body. Mental massage, however,
doesn't employ any such aids. Bodily attentiveness is the only
instrument of observation. Thirdly, magnetism's eighteenth
century view that the will to recovery is a natural drive
on the part of the organism. Fourthly, the Buddha's great
speech on the *Foundations of Consciousness* – inclusive of

attentiveness to the body, permitting, among other things, the tranquil, unrestricted flow of the breath. Zen meditation is also concerned with that. And fifthly, the Chinese moving meditation of T'ai Chi, furthering polar experience of the body. I'll first describe directed mental massage, and then – in a brief second section – improvised mental massage.

Directed mental massage also helps acquaint people with the many body sensations that can be awoken through this process. Once that has been achieved, we are free to leave the main path from time to time, and to follow a newly sensed way of our own in improvised mental massage. If we were to stick to a fixed procedure, there would be a danger of mental massage becoming alienated as an external ritual, and thus ineffective. Returning to the main path in directed mental massage is nevertheless especially helpful at times of crisis and strain when spontaneous sensing is blocked. But even in directed mental massage it's important to proceed intuitively – that is, to allow physical sensations to happen, sensing them from within, rather than wilfully producing them.

We lie comfortably on the back with arms and legs loosely outstretched, the head facing upwards (that is, not turned to the side), and the eyes closed. We attempt to relax our muscles so far as is already possible. This muscular relaxation and the breathing will deepen of their own accord during the course of the mental massage. Attention shouldn't therefore be mainly directed towards them. Now we turn relaxed awareness towards the palms of the hands. That doesn't mean willpower and deliberate concentration, but rather unconditional inner attention, comparable with what we, forgetting our ego, direct towards a face that absolutely appeals to us, casting its spell. It is as if this inner awareness were attracted by the part of the body involved.

Now we simply wait and see what happens in the palms of our hands. They will probably soon become warm, start to tingle pleasantly, and begin to vibrate gently with the intensified flow of blood. The cat begins to purr. We only move on when sensations in the palms diminish slightly after previous intensification. Then we slowly move our attention down both arms simultaneously, always remaining where feelings are greater. Intensive sensations of pulling and flowing – sometimes linked with a real bubbling as

145

often occurs in the legs to an even greater extent – can develop in the veins at the level of the elbows. By directing attention to such sensations so far as possible, we leave no space for distracting thoughts. It is as if our body could at last – thanks to our non-purposive attention – unfold its own life and movement, as if it had been released from slavery to aim-oriented will and was now able to implement those little 'useless' movements needed for its health in the same way as a child requires space to play. When the relaxed muscles also start to react, we sense that particularly clearly. The muscles in the upper arm, followed by the chest muscles and then the heart muscle (in conjunction with the left chest muscle), now start to move in a pleasurably playful and unpredictable fashion, beyond the work for which they are made, and loosen up with these autonomous movements which are sometimes like slight twitches. In the heart muscle, these subtle autonomous movements, which are independent of the performance involved in the heartbeat, lead to a relaxed, sure sense of well being.

CONTRA-INDICATIONS

We allow such movements to die away on their own, and don't attempt to strengthen them through additional will-power, which would result in muscular tension rather than relaxation. The reason for additional willpower is often fear of what simply happens without our interference. Should such muscular tension occur in the heart, which is highly unlikely and can only happen if spontaneous attention doesn't work, we immediately abandon mental massage of the heart area so as not to harm ourselves physically. We should also do so in the case of nervous disruption of the heart rhythm, which very occasionally occurs if we think of other things – obligations, and so on – whilst doing the mental massage. If a slight tension develops in any other muscle apart from the heart, we attempt to transform the inappropriate willpower into impartial and non-directive attention. If that's successful, the tense muscle loosens and starts moving powerfully, as if overwhelmed with gratitude. Well-being now streams from this muscle throughout the body.

The normal reaction to muscular tension is directed defensively against the place affected, isolating it from the organism as a whole: resistance against resistance. That very separation strengthens the tension because it reduces the blood supply. That connection can easily be observed in a cramp in the calf muscles. As soon as we become aware of such anxious protectiveness and instead devote loving attentiveness to the place affected, the cramp or tension usually dissolves within a short time, and pleasurable life then pulses with the blood though where the pain was felt. It is once again linked up with the body as a whole. Sportsmen can thus also deploy local mental massage to overcome fears of muscular cramps or pain resulting from over-exertion, increasing the performance of the muscle now reunited with the entire organism. They should of course also do what they normally do in the case of such problems.

We have now moved from the hands slowly up the arms to the shoulders, and have started descending the front side of the body. Among many people, women as well as men, both sides of the chest respond powerfully to mental massage. Nervous people, inhibited in their relationships, particularly feel powerful and loving well-being here, spreading in waves to the entire body. Fantasies of love can develop in the process. We just let them come and go again. This well-being intensifies if we allow our attention to be simultaneously directed towards both sides of the chest. It's as if electric current pulses between these two poles of which we are now aware. Mental massage is therefore stimulating as well as relaxing. During our travels through the body, the poles can be more or less distant from one another, but polar awareness is always beneficial. We experience the field between the two poles as being charged with energy, as a sphere tingling and vibrating with life.

We now imagine that the poles on both sides of the chest come ever closer, uniting at the centre of power beneath the breast bone (known in Tantrism as the heart chakra) just as if we are slowly and with great concentration moving our two clenched fists towards each other, experiencing our strength in the field in between. That place can be the source of much autonomous movement in the body. It's as if our body were beaten like a gong at this point. The attention directed towards it would be the mallet. Vibrations spread in ever larger circles. Polar consciousness persists even if the two poles are now united. This is no longer expressed, as previously, in attraction, but in a striving to separate as if the entire chest wanted to expand from its centre out into space. We sense dynamic spaciousness and our breathing gets deeper. Here too we shouldn't rush. Persistence in attentiveness intensifies the healing sensations. That applies to all phases within mental massage.

If this autonomous movement also diminishes, we allow attention to slide downwards across the front of the body, spreading over the stomach. The stomach often begins to rumble in the first seconds and at the same time to move in various places as if it were being massaged by an invisible hand. The cat purrs with a mounting sense of well-being. We simply follow those places in the stomach where life makes itself most intensely felt, and remain there. We gradually begin to feel as if we had just awoken from a refreshing midday sleep. The intestines now also begin to move here and there because of the increased blood supply. Once again we attentively follow the body, which is our guide. Being in the intestines deepens the feeling that all is well in the body. Attention now gradually moves on to the sexual organs. Here too we're not pursuing any specific purpose such as sexual stimulation and excitement. We allow the pleasurable vibrations to come and go as they wish. Sometimes they're stronger, sometimes weaker. That's of no importance.

WORKING ON THE LOWER BODY

The poles of consciousness are once again clearly separated when attention moves slowly down the front of both legs, pausing here and there. An enjoyably charged energy field develops between them. Apart from the muscles' autonomous movement, the unblocking bubbling of the blood in the veins made more elastic by relaxation is sensed particularly strongly here. Many people feel the freeing of the flow of blood and life through bi-polar attentiveness more intensely in the back of the knee and later the ankles. We now stroke the top of the foot down to the tips of the toes, and then turn to the soles. This is the switching-point between the descending and the ascending movement within awareness of the body. The soles of the feet are exceptionally charged places of power. It's worth dwelling there for a longer period. Initial attention is often enough to cause a wave of fierce energy to shoot up from the feet along the legs and throughout the entire body. We shouldn't strengthen that sudden boost in energy through additional willpower, but must rather remain with the soles of the feet. Powerful rapid sensations are then replaced by intensely inward feelings. The former indicated how unconsciously we normally stand on our feet, that is on the earth and the ground of reality.

The rising movement of attention goes through the rear half of the body. When we slowly proceed up the legs to the buttocks, we sense how our well-being develops and becomes ever more comprehensive. The sensations in the front of the body haven't, however, vanished. Even if they have diminished again, they still vibrate within the organism as a whole. Self-love expands, expressing itself in an ever more complete vibration involving the entire body. We encircle the buttocks from all sides until we pleasantly sense their roundness. Then we cautiously start climbing the back, pausing where life 'resonates' more strongly. At the level of the kidneys the poles of attention become more clearly separate until a warm tingling spreads from the back around the entire trunk. We move up along the back, following our sensations, restricting and expanding polar attentiveness as seems beneficial.

We'll probably stay longer in the neck because it is a place of strong sensations – sometimes initially painful, but then loosening and relaxing. By opening ourselves to these sensations rather than avoiding them, we link the head with its thoughts to the body as a whole. We now continue by mounting the back of the head up to the crown. Here we perhaps feel as if we were being magnetically attracted from a point above the top of the head. If we sense that, our breathing will become even deeper than it already has during the course of this mental massage. We now allow our attention to spread across the face and the entire head. The skin tingles as if secretly caressed. Finally, we fill the body as a whole with our attention for as long and profoundly as possible. The totality of the body vibrates like a purring cat. Previously silent, isolated areas are now linked up and hum along with this 'resonant body'. These body vibrations do not stop at the skin. They also extend to the outer world. Self-love becomes love of the other. The newly invigorated energy radiates. Mental massage, which may at first sight have seemed to intensify narcissistic isolation, ultimately turns out to be a way leading to liberation from an ego that fearfully shuts itself off from a vital relationship with the outer world. Mental massage attains its natural conclusion in the experience of self-love merging with love of the other. The completeness of the process on this or that occasion is unimportant. All that matters is the feeling of having entered upon a process entailing self-liberation and self-healing.

I mentioned at the start that we shouldn't limit ourselves to directed mental massage. Even if it does make possible many intense and unexpected experiences along the way, it remains overall a pre-established model. As such it can deprive the body of a degree of initiative. But trust in our body expresses itself in the very fact that we do completely entrust it with initiative, allowing ourselves to be guided by its movements. The basic path in mental massage is often useful, but under certain circumstances it may not provide complete liberation from anxiety. Directed mental massage must therefore be complemented by the improvised form.

Our dreams impress us so much because they arise spontaneously out of the depths of our being – even if they may be influenced by external factors such as residues of daily experiences. Like dreams, bodily sensations give us – in improvised rather than in guided mental massage – the intensive feeling of being completely present within ourselves, liberated from imposed ideas and intentions. That feeling, which furthers authentic experience of ourselves, helps us to gradually become free from such dependences of which we are still ignorant today.

RELEASING REPRESSED SENSATIONS

Comprehended in that profound way, mental massage isn't just an exercise. Like dream memories it comes within the competence of depth psychology. Hitherto repressed and repulsed bodily sensations make themselves known.

Life takes place if we allow that. Being present in the body, as furthered by mental massage, is also part of a comprehensively viewed depth psychology. Bodily sensations arise even before dream images. In the womb we experience such sensations but probably not dreams. The body that is conscious of itself is the human being's original awareness. We shy away from this awareness because it also entails transience and death. But we thereby cheat ourselves of the vital pleasure that only comes from the body. The separation of body therapy and depth psychology is artificial and harmful. Body therapy thus becomes instructions for physical exercise, which betray improvisation – the spirit that bloweth where it listeth – and depth psychology a thought process blocking bodily energies.

In improvised mental massage, unlike the directed form, we expect the initial and all subsequent signs of life to come directly from the body. We don't therefore direct attention to the sensations occurring in pre-selected parts of the body – for example, the palms of the two hands – but instead allow the body itself to move as it wishes, both now and in all that follows. Perhaps a pain in a specific place first becomes apparent. In that case we devote all our attention to that place without rejecting or isolating it. The pain is neither positive nor negative. It is simply 'right as it is'. It's what we are. Our alert attentiveness thus becomes identical with it. That is probably what is meant by the unfortunately phrased demand that we 'accept' a pain. Taken literally, it would be masochistic simply to accept a pain since that would signify that we override our feelings in taking on something alien that doesn't belong to us. If we merely 'accept' a pain as if it flew in from outside, nothing would happen except perhaps for us becoming depressed or seeking some religious superstructure such as belief in a suffering God and a pain-free eternity. If, however, we experience ourselves within this unrejected pain, unexpectedly much happens. During mental massage the pain resulting from tension often rapidly dissolves, making way for a great many spontaneous bodily movements and sensations. An increase in the energy level and the flow rate of the blood and other bodily liquids, and the liberated autonomous life of the muscles and inner organs, receive expression in an unbelievable vitalisation. The energy pulsates, trickles, gurgles, is dammed for a while, and then rushes onwards all the more powerfully. Those expressions are not metaphors for the sensations of a liberated body, but are words of experience, forcing themselves onto our lips when our body undergoes liberation through the dissolution of pain and tension. Sensation returns of its own accord to a specific part of the body. Attention shifts spontaneously since a new body sensation, pleasant or unpleasant, arises in another unexpected place. Improvised mental massage moves through the body, following the occurrence of sensations. Relaxed attentiveness follows those sensations without pursuing any particular objective. Bodily sensations usually become more pleasurable as mental massage continues. Nonetheless, even the first bodily stirrings can be agreeable. We shouldn't therefore seek pain that isn't there.

If we have sufficient time, we should prolong this wandering through the body for as long as awareness is attracted to different parts. That applies to both directed and improvised mental massage. If there's little time at our disposal, a few minutes are often enough for vitalisation. The polar experience in improvised mental massage doesn't result (as in the directed form) from simultaneous direction of attention to both poles – for instance, the two hands – but rather from the field of tension between the part of the body we've just felt most strongly and is now slowly getting less intense, and another part where sensations are becoming ever more apparent.

The relaxed attitude of lying is most conducive to mental massage, but this can also be pursued when sitting or walking slowly. Body attention also slowly extends to periods when we are not 'practising'. Mental massage as a special 'practice' then increasingly gives way to general bodily attentiveness – just as someone used to living consciously with his dreams doesn't have to interpret every single one in order to be in touch with the depths of being where dreams originate.

HEALING EFFECT

It seems as if mental massage also maintains health and furthers convalescence in those organs which are less liable to cramps and tensions. If our body becomes a purring cat, impulses promoting recovery emanate from the entire body's sense of well-being to the individual organs, muscles, and vessels. The pleasurable inner 'purring' we otherwise only know from gratifying sexual encounters exerts a healing impact.

Intensive sensations, which direct our attention to areas cut off from the flow of life, often develop around parts of the body – mute, dulled, hard, dead – which don't respond to directed or improvised mental massage. Such parts of the body, which we experience as having 'dropped out', indicate a deep-rooted physical complex. A sexual complex expresses itself as muteness and numbness within that sphere. Legs that were made fun of during childhood remain as lifeless as wood, and so on. These dead body areas are zones of lovelessness, and areas where self-love is lacking.

Hypochondriacs, who suggest all possible illnesses to themselves and for that reason perhaps really succumb one day, learn from the relaxed, impartial attentiveness of mental massage to pick up the body's real messages. They no longer see the body as an enemy, but through devotion of attention become identical with it. The sickness-inducing separation from the body entailed in fears of illness has thus been overcome.

Mental massage furthers instinctive self-healing and spontaneous 'self-correction' (Feldenkrais). Intuitive experience of the body leads to the melting and digestion of cramps, tensions, and wrong postures (Boyesen). Recovery results from linking up with the energy in pain rather than violently overcoming or suppressing it. We achieve that link through renouncing any negative evaluation and affirming tranquil attentiveness. The pain can now dissolve itself and change into a new focus of energy. The hypochondriac's destructive distrust of his or her body is transformed in mental massage into healing sensitivity.

A few minutes of mental massage are often enough for us to feel fresh and relaxed. If we need sleep, it furthers the relaxation needed for falling asleep. It also counters disturbances of sleep. If we go to sleep again after mental massage, pleasurable, life-affirming dreams occur astonishingly often.

Mental massage acts along the erotic trail, dissolving traumatic unloved games through devoting attention to the reality of what is happening in the body. It heals by freeing the possibility of a new, growth-promoting existence.

FOURTEEN

Love Is Abnormal

'Erotic emotion explodes the established structures with which the ego has hitherto identified itself whether those be of a more famililial and social or a more individual nature'[1], I wrote in *How to Say No to the One You Love*. Love explodes norms. Initially the norms taken over from the original family – how one thinks and feels. The person loved is different, calls myself in question, and makes my life more expansive. Then love bursts the norms upheld by social conventions, and thus my reactive adaptation to what others expect and demand of me. When I'm in love my own needs push and pull me. Finally, it overthrows the norms the individual with his fears and uncertainties has imposed on himself. Love makes you courageous, allowing you to act freely and venture on the unknown.

At the start love can be like the big bang, a sudden explosion from within sweeping away the restraints, established over many years, of restricted views and subdued feelings, and opening up the horizon all around as it expands outwards in wave-like pulsations. If we allow ourselves to be drawn into the initial spontaneous movement, consciously taking it further, it will gradually lead us, despite occasional rearguard action, to a new fundamental attitude: the *erotic attitude*. We are then instinctively always about to lift a curtain, break through a wall, transform unchangeable ideas into mere viewpoints, and play around with all aspects of sacrosanct norms until they crumble and are replaced by new, more appropriate, but equally provisional norms. Love creates unforeseen new links. It can easily and quickly annul decisions we carefully calculated and planned within our former limits.

The Latin word 'norma' from which the English word 'norm' derives signifies 'square, rule, guideline, regulation'.

The Wound of the Unloved

A norm is thus something collectively envisaged and prescribed, uniformly expected of many individuals. It aims at upholding what is given whereas love bursts bounds. Love is abnormal to the extent that it potentially annuls all norms, which doesn't, however, mean that we must infringe laws in order to be able to love. Anyone who affirms love's instinctive urge achieves emancipation and liberation in all spheres. Norms have lost their absolute power over him or her. Loving and liberating are the same thing.

ORGANISED RATHER THAN LOVED

Unloved children are often subjected to the pressure of parental norms, which is stronger than their love. They're organised rather than loved, which is particularly clear in the case of the inhabitants of children's homes. From the people bringing them up they experience restrictive rules of behaviour and soulless incorporation in a social machine, or are left to themselves, instead of experiencing spontaneous expressions of feeling which could communicate vital impulses. Gestures of love are rarer and weaker than aim-oriented manipulation. The parents may be too fearful to entrust themselves to their urge to give love; they may also see the child as too much of a nuisance to be able to open their hearts; they may feel that too much is expected of them, and merely maintain the child as with a machine, allowing their feelings to atrophy and their offspring to be emotionally deprived; or they may, as the outcome of having themselves been unloved, perpetuate the general chain of lovelessness. Such children aren't loved but merely looked after in terms of specific norms. All too seldom do they experience that fixed meal times can be broken, and that parents respond to unhappiness by taking them warmly and reassuringly in their arms, or share their happiness, thereby increasing the child's. Norms are stronger than love.

Later in their life the unloved thus feel themselves under the constant pressure of a loveless expectation or demand. That is accompanied by an enormous inner urge to explode the normative corset in which they are suffocating. To begin with, that urge is not lived out. But if they fall in love with someone, they may finally succeed in breaking through the

156

norms that have prevailed in their life to date. But the way in which they experience liberation from these norms also involves an element of tragedy. Against their background of past suffering, love is not primarily viewed as liberation *towards* another human being whose otherness became a model for their own still fallow existential possibilities. It is more likely to be seen as liberation *from* enslavement to life-inhibiting norms, as liberation from the past rather than directed towards the future. For such people love is initially a sign of old chains falling away and out of date norms being destroyed. Hardly any energy is left for developing a new life.

That is why the unloved, who have not comprehended and liberated themselves from their childhood fate, experience unhappy love-relationships. When the pressure from within breaks through, they now overshoot the mark where the suffering was greatest. If, for instance, a woman was ignored and pushed aside by her father, as an adult she perhaps tends towards excessively caring for and spoiling her partner – as she would have liked to have been treated by her father during childhood – until he responds to her over-extravagant love with lovelessness, that is mounting demands and finally estrangement. She wanted to annul the norm of a functional relationship as practised by her father, and once again finds herself in a relationship increasingly characterised by delimitation and the partner's hurtful behaviour. She falls back into her childhood fate of living with an unloving man.

The unloved caught up in this unfortunate pattern time and again exclude themselves from love. I remember a man whose strongest feeling during childhood and adolescence was of constant rivalry with his father, who criticised, found fault with, and punished his son almost unceasingly. My acquaintance's life was nothing but a struggle against his father, directed towards conquering the mother. The Oedipus complex develops in such a family constellation. Later in his life this man regularly fell in love with women who were weary of their marriages but he was more concerned with freeing himself from a dominant father than with loving these ladies. Constriction by the father was stronger than his longing for the mother. The father became a token of all the norms opposing the son's life-force. Liberating himself from

157

his father was this man's most important concern. Taking away another man's wife was a symbolic action with which he sought to flee the unbearable pressure of his own fate. He wanted to destroy an institution, namely a marriage, in order to cancel out the norm he saw his father as embodying. To start with, most women went along with his game. Those periods constituted the only happy times in his life. He could succumb to the illusion of at last ridding himself of his family fate – of putting his 'father' out of action and marrying his 'mother'. But he always set up his relationship with these women weary of marriage in such a way that it finally broke down. These women, stimulated by the adventure with my acquaintance, returned to the old marriage with renewed self-confidence. The father thus triumphed once again, and the family destiny was confirmed. In one instance, however, there was a divorce, and it seemed as if my friend had at last freed himself from his father. That made him so grateful that he happily submitted to his partner in everything. But her reaction to such subordination was to increasingly pursue the same power game as his father had played without my friend realising how he had helped bring that about. Seeking freedom from his father he once again lost his mother's love, and rediscovered himself as enslaved to the father, now embodied by his partner. He excluded himself from love because he couldn't really free himself from his father. His childhood norm triumphed over abnormal love.

THE PROMISE OF FREEDOM

In all cases love explodes early existential norms. But if those were extremely powerful during childhood, after a while they catch up with love and destroy it. Only a love that principally involves liberation towards something new, a vital movement pushing into the unknown rather than destruction of what is already known, can fulfil the promise of freedom.

There are many examples of that in literature. In Kleist's tragedy *Penthesilea*, for instance, the main character's chief reason for love is the negative one of wanting to destroy an inhuman norm: the Amazons' law of only giving themselves to a man conquered in battle whom chance brought their

way. If norms hostile to life predominate in a person's existence, a completely unconscious striving is directed towards
destroying them. Love is then nothing but an instrument of
this destruction. It thus remains caught up within the system, fixated on the old norms. Real love, on the other hand,
provides its own justification. It isn't directed *against* norms
but instead relativises them *within* its own exuberant vital
movement. Love isn't directed against norms. It is *anormal*,
that is beyond unchangeable norms' claim to absolute right.
Love transforms norms into changeable rules within a game
subordinate to life. But norms that turn out to be stronger
than love destroy it. That is why Penthesilea finally kills her
lover Achilles whom she had chosen for herself in defiance
of the Amazon norm. Achilles initially signifies Penthesilea's
liberation from the norm but its power is ultimately confirmed in her act of madness. The unloved tend towards
being time and again overwhelmed by norms that bring about
illness. If that happens, they become increasingly embroiled
in the state of being unloved. Love remains unlived.

The same experience is undergone by Christians who have
not learnt to feel the actual strength of their flesh – beyond
normative belief in the weakness of the flesh (Paul) – and
bodily pleasure beyond all norms, and to follow their natural
lust for life. Their lack of self-love inclusive of the body, and
the oppression of their rejection of the flesh, leads them
to self-renunciatory love of neighbour. There they go way
beyond the mark because they unconsciously want to liberate themselves from the oppression of an existence lacking
genuine self-love. That's why they ultimately fall again into
the old prison of lack of freedom, sadness, and depression.

For Confucius, the Chinese philosopher, love never involved blind and destructive self-renunciation, which doesn't
help one's fellows. A brief dialogue between Zai Wo and
Confucius illustrated that. Zai Wo says: 'If someone full of
love (Chinese: ren) is told that another person has fallen into
a deep well, he'll probably rush to throw himself in too'.
Confucius answers: 'But why on earth should he do that?
Someone reasonable might go to the well but he wouldn't
throw himself in'.[2] He will do all he can to bring about a
rescue, but not plunge into the same misfortune out of blind
sympathy. The supposed love of neighbour vanishes amid

identification with the unfortunate, and the old feeling of being unloved spreads anew. That explains the frequency of depression among people who for lack of love plunge into love of neighbour as a source of pleasure. Love is, however, indivisible. Anyone who excludes himself from love completely loses it.

The fact that self-love and love of neighbour belong together has become a commonplace, but it remains nothing but words so long as the bodily experience of love's indivisibility is lacking. Love of self and of one's neighbour don't just belong together; they are identical. In a sexual encounter love is greatest when the pleasure I give becomes my own pleasure. In that respect love is like a peaceful contest involving pleasure in a mutual game. I can only prevail in a contest if I focus on my centre and don't lose balance. If, however, I rush towards my opponent, I do lose my centre – and as a result of that eccentricity become the loser. The techniques used in Far Eastern martial arts deploy the wisdom of fighting with your opponent's strength as well as your own. If I should nevertheless lose, I don't feel humiliated since my opponent's victory is also a triumph for my own strength. Feelings of powerlessness and a craving for revenge cannot develop within myself if my opponent and I constitute one and the same play of energies. In a peaceful struggle the opponent becomes a friend with whom I am united in a polar dance of energies: 'Beneath the contest lies friendship'.[3] The situation is the same with love of neighbour. If I lose, thereby betraying myself, impotent feelings of anger and destruction arise in the unconscious. That's why specialists in love of neighbour are eaten up by rivalry, greed for power, and intolerance. Anyone, on the other hand, who maintains his balance and rests in his centre can struggle and love joyously.

ABNORMAL LOVE BECOMING POSSIBLE

Norms are transformed into rules of the game in the uniting spirit of play. They lose the rigidity and absolute claims that obstruct vital movement. An abnormal love now becomes possible. An absolute norm, an absolute morality, and an absolute 'Thou shalt' always signify separation from life and a loss of self-love. The need for security is satisfied for a while, but then depression grows. The unloved, who hope for love as a result of their submission to norms, rediscover themselves in the 'normal' feeling of being unloved. But if the gesture involved in my embracing and giving love is a gesture of my own delight in life, norms are changed into linguistic rules, into a 'grammar of feeling', making possible understanding and shared activity as agreements leading to the establishment of association.

A deterrent morality and legislation are said to be necessary because of the existence of an enormous amount of hatred and destructiveness – but these harmful feelings can be largely transformed into peaceful and uniting feelings of contest and measurement of strength. Depth psychology's most important social contribution entails making possible a culture of love within many individuals, and giving expression to the norm-surmounting energy processes involved in love. How that should come to pass is the theme of this entire book. I'll clarify my concern by analysing a dream. A young man dreamt that he stood in front of a wooden barrier behind which he saw two dead horses and a woman. He at first assumed she was dead too. Then he noticed how she lifted her right hand and summoned him through an opening in the barricade. But he allowed a group of people to drag him away from the woman. In the next dream sequence an unknown person stood in front of an open window, ready to jump out and kill himself. The dreamer tried to stop him. Then he woke up.

This young man was worried about erotic relationships with the result that his feelings for women were mostly anaesthetised and dead. He protected himself with a barrier against his own vitality, symbolised by the two dead horses. Dreams often indicate the way the life-force is striving. This dream tempts the dreamer to pass through a barrier, a long-established norm, and to thrust forward to a love free of norms. The woman – his capacity for relationships with women – isn't yet completely dead, even if his instinctive powers, the horses, may seem to be lifeless. He can save the woman and heal himself. The drive towards self-healing is at work within himself. The woman signals that he should come to her. But anonymous, that is unconscious, powers – the group that pulls him back – are still stronger. The unwritten norm, determined by his reaction against a cold mother – 'No real love exists between woman and man' – dominates once again. Since, however, he has just perceived the possibility of at long last coming to life in love (the alluring woman), his discouragement through a renewed retreat becomes dangerously absolute. That is demonstrated by the unknown (that is unconscious for the young man) would-be suicide. Leaping to death would be a continuation of the negative momentum away from love into self-destruction. The dead horses wouldn't be resurrected and the woman wouldn't wave again. The unloved man would himself complete his destiny. Suicide would bring him freedom *from* the norm but wouldn't take him *towards* vitality. The dream leaves the man with the task of preventing this catastrophe.

The dreamer is still following the traumatic trail. The burden of norms hostile to life becomes so heavy that he would like to allow himself to fall to his death. But the erotic pattern – the woman striving for connection – has flashed into awareness. Dreams are fragments of fantasy that can be complemented and made more complete whilst one is in a waking state. That doesn't happen through suggestions from the therapist. It occurs when the therapist and client together pursue the erotic pattern, constantly paying attention to the latter's own inner relationship to this pattern whether this be expressed in words or not. In a climate of healing relationship, the client increasingly experiences fantasies which tempt towards life – both in dreams and during waking hours. Incorporating such fantasies in everyday language and everyday activities strengthens zest and momentum on the erotic trail. Dead norms cannot be analysed out of existence, but only relativised in the experience of abnormal love and made accessible to change. There thus occurs a liberation resulting from an inner drive that doesn't have to be paid for with death – a love that is identification with what wants to live. And yet the range of *élan vital* present in any human being remains a mystery. Not all weariness of life should be viewed as being pathological. Nevertheless, as long as norms oppress us, energy is still striving for vital expression, and love wants to break open a barrier, a restriction on life, dissolving a constricting and burdensome norm, and opening and unburdening us.

FIFTEEN

Essential Solitude

The unloved think they've been abandoned by the entire world. They don't know that they abandon themselves. Those two sentences summarise all the examples in the preceding chapter to the extent those showed that clinging to the family's fate and blocking self-love bring about abandonment, the same abandonment which tormented the unloved during childhood. As soon as we grasp that the crux of the matter lies in self-abandonment and separation from one's own essence – and not in being abandoned by others – we start changing our line of vision. We look inwards more than outwards. We expect less in the way of care and attention from outside, contenting ourselves with clearing away the obstacles to self-love and self-healing. No longer fixated on the external world but now inwardly oriented, we feel an impulse from within rather than pressure from outside. We no longer seek someone else's resources but become our own source of vitality. We no longer experience solitude as abandonment but as the fountainhead of our capacity to love. I thus turn first in this chapter to that loneliness which oppresses and isolates, and then to the solitude that liberates and unites. I call the latter essential solitude since it leads to maturation and our essential being unfolds there if we know how to use it.

'Your bad love of yourselves makes solitude a prison for you'.[1] People who can't put up with themselves and succumb to lack of initiative and restlessness as soon as they are alone, people who don't like themselves enough to feel at ease in their own company, are prisoners of lack of love for themselves. They restlessly roam the world in search of someone who has the key for opening their prison from outside. They seek new friends, new lovers, new therapists, new ideological leaders, teachers, masters, gurus, and lamas, who are supposed to reveal the secret of the crucial word and to free them from isolation. But the prison door can only be opened from within, and they themselves are the key. Liberation from imprisonment in the ego begins with love of self.

BUDDHIST IDEOLOGY

We who have grown up and become deformed within the Judaeo-Christian tradition have problems with that paradox. We suspect that imprisonment in the ego lies behind self-love, and egocentricity behind solitude. The opposite is true. Real self-love liberates from the ego, and essential solitude creates capacity for love. My objective in this chapter is to demonstrate that, and to put an end, at long last, to the misrepresentation that the Buddhist neglects love of his fellow creatures by being turned inwards. In Buddhism's Great Vehicle the central ethical value is 'Bodhicitta', the illumination of the heart from which wells sympathy for all suffering beings. Reverence for the Bodhisattvas – the future Buddhas whose objective is through compassion to free others from suffering – is of great importance. In Buddhist countries we find particularly much warm, undemanding love for the other, rooted in vitalisation of one's own heart, but not 'eccentric' love of neighbour which also does things the other should do for himself, deriving psychologically from lack of self-love and a repressed greed for power. In Buddhism there doesn't exist any idea of redemption from outside – only self-liberation. That entails love and liberation from imprisonment in the ego. That paradox can only be grasped by way of personal experience.

People who were abandoned early and unloved are isolated and lack partners. They do to themselves what others have done to them. They leave themselves in the lurch (see chapter 8). Having rejected themselves, they no longer know anyone who could love them. Someone who loses all sense of himself or herself cannot be a lover or a partner. This absence of relationship with another makes a person a prisoner of his or her own unloved ego.

The way towards essential solitude always leads through suffering from isolation and abandonment. No one is completely spared that. Suffering is a necessary part of growth. 'Only when pain is felt does the search begin'.[2] Either unfortunate circumstances really do lead to early abandonment, or the feeling of not being understood, accepted, and loved develops quite naturally during the necessary stages of separation. I'll present an example of both possibilities. The sense of a link between various cases of abandonment can lead someone unloved and left in the lurch at an early age to feel that this isolation, brought about by particular circumstances, involves an archetypal core of experience common to all people.

Martin Buber, the Jewish philosopher, was abandoned at an early age. When he was three, his parents separated and he was sent to his father's parents. Here he was looked after by an older girl. Buber writes in an autobiographical fragment:

> I cannot remember that I ever spoke about my mother to my more experienced companion. But I can still hear how this big girl said to me: 'No, she'll never come back'. I know that I remained silent, but also that I did not have the least doubt about the truth of what had been said. It stuck in my mind, from year to year increasingly establishing itself in my heart, but after about ten years I had started to feel that this was something affecting everyone, and not just me . . . I assume that any form of true encounter I experienced during the course of my life originated in that moment on the balcony.[3]

The background of early abandonment and isolation makes particularly clear what applies to every human being. Encounter and relationship are experiences at the limits, not something to be taken for granted. On the one hand is 'the world that doesn't rhyme with Mother', as Sloterdijk once said: the world into which we feel ourselves to be thrown, born too early, insecure, abandoned, and unloved. On the other is the world of relationships, of arms opening and eyes meeting. Love can only flourish on the borderline between these two worlds. A balance is here mutually maintained and annulled between the pessimism of one world and the optimism of the other. This is the place of a love amazed at itself.

It is not just in separation and abandonment, but also in the natural course of development of our lives, that a hitherto familiar world becomes alien to us. Even now we sense an abyss of isolation and lack of love for ourselves. Almost all novels concerned with puberty demonstrate that.[4] In his novel *Agostino*, Alberto Moravia, the Italian author, describes the sufferings involved in the thirteen year-old hero's breaking away from his mother. Agostino had previously mistakenly believed that their lives were absolutely attuned, and that she had no autonomous existence separating her from him. But at a Mediterranean seaside town he witnesses how she passionately loves a young man, Renzo. 'It dawned on him . . . that his mother is also a woman, perhaps determined by feelings that exclude him'. This insight compels him to break away from his mother. Thrown back on himself, he feels alone and contemptible, but at the same time he discovers his own sensuality. He thus needs the pain of isolation so as to become aware of his own urge towards love. In the moment when he crosses the frontier between the world of being unloved and the world of love, a 'planned' developmental leap takes place in his life.

EXPERIENCING 'OTHERNESS'

In such moments we experience our *otherness* – not just as compared to our mother or another person from whom we are beginning to distinguish ourselves, but also with regard to our previous ideas about ourself. 'I is another' writes Jacques Lacan (see chapter 8) – not just now and by chance, but always and essentially. The two worlds of familiarity and strangeness are within ourselves. In the feeling of strangeness both love of another and self-love are a leap into the void. We never completely know who we are loving there. Every fresh clarification is accompanied by renewed obscuration. Enlightenment can never be achieved because it is simultaneously confusion. One eye sees a new order, the other renewed disorder. With one hand we establish a relationship, and with the other we indicate the abyss that separates. If we comprehend both simultaneously, accepting them as they are, our abandonment is transformed into a solitude in which we unfold our capacity for love of the other.

Let us now look more closely at our otherness – at the world of the other within ourselves, making us seem strange to ourselves and our fellows, at the existential aspect of being unloved and essential solitude. Everything that is alien arouses anxiety because it touches on the wound of solitude, moving us where we would like to be unmoved and concealed. If somebody reveals – contrary to our wishes – whatever is alien within ourselves, we feel rejected and unhappy. But if we ourselves decide to expose our otherness because we can no longer bear isolation, love, happiness, and a sense of freedom flood through us – sometimes even when we meet with lack of understanding from someone in whom we have confided. We have broken through the decisive isolation, summoning up the courage to be different, and through this revelation have transformed what was most shameful into the greatest treasure.

Some people feel such an urgent impulse towards self-revelation that they even stake their life, so essential does communication of what was most concealed seem to them. In Max Frisch's *Andorra*, the prevalent mania in Andri's everyday world – the demonisation of the Jews – thus becomes his greatest wish: 'I want to be other'. He may not really be a Jew, no matter what the people around him think, but for him being a Jew becomes a symbol of genuine difference, of a secret and a primary value. Dying for that signifies more life than continuing to exist as a conformist. Andri is thus taken away to be exterminated in the great pogrom. This inevitable fate is at the same time his essential freedom.

I sometimes have the impression that people who confide a secret in me as their psychotherapist actually mean something else – a state of being different that can't be expressed in words, something primordially unfamiliar, a pure mystery that isn't an insoluble riddle. This existential otherness, which is not completely reducible to any concrete statement, vainly seeks experiences and facts allowing for self-expression. Today anyone can tell some story from his or her life which is believed to provide a key to their entire existence. A few weeks later he or she tells a different story, which now seems to contain the crucial revelation. And so on. Such attempts at explanation repress the existential aspect of solitude or being unloved, involving being thrown into an alien world, and feeling oneself to have been born too soon and plunged into unfamiliar depths without any support and security. He or she would like to outwit this state of being radically other by exposing secret after secret from within, thereby seeking support through putting into words what has become graspable. But his renewed seeking for fresh explanations demonstrates that what he means is beyond explanation. Andri is not a Jew, but he gives his life for his otherness which cannot be described more closely.

If we recognise and accept the dimension of our otherness, thereby conceding that we don't have everything under control but constantly derail ourselves without therefore being schizoid or even psychotic, then something absolutely remarkable happens to us. We unite with the world and start to love. An unbelievable, radical liberation takes place when we no longer conceal our existential state of being unloved and insecure, our essential solitude, and even make that the launching pad for our existence. The paradox is unsurpassable. We allow ourselves, from the depths of our being, to fall into the reality of being unloved and lost without the least degree of detachment as observers, and for the first time we become completely united with the world as beloved and lover in one person.

A SINGLE SOLITUDE

Is that paradox really so strange? Isn't being consciously other identical with liberation from an ego-consciousness that has isolated us from the other within ourselves and the world as well as from other people? Doesn't solitude basically involve contact with other solitaries, and union within the inaccessible, the spontaneous, and the wordless mystery – rather than in what is known, in established habits and conventions of thought, and in the long-entrenched and definitively recorded? Love springs up between two solitudes like a spark of understanding without comprehension, an intensity of feeling without explicable feelings, or a liberation without there being any initial change of life-situation. This love derives from the insight that all solitudes are one, that there only exists a *single* solitude, a *single* shared abyss, a *single* falling silent, and a *single* void. Insight into the underlying identity of being loved and unloved, of relationship and solitude, is the event that frees us to become human.

Individual otherness, such as belonging to a different race, some kind of handicap, an affliction, sexual interests opposing the norm, left-handedness, and outstanding talent, or a despised vice, points towards every human being's *fundamental otherness*. It is important to become identified with one's individual otherness so as to devote loving attention towards this particular treasure. In order, however, to avoid isolation it is equally important to see the fundamental otherness behind that, the essential solitude which we share with all other human beings. The obvious differentness of a specific person signals the existence of an existential otherness and strangeness. If we could creep into someone else's skin, we would rediscover that otherness. That insight is also of significance for psychology because we are tempted to want to cover up and surmount existential facts by way of therapy.

A colleague told me about a married transvestite who suffered from his wife's refusal to see and admire him dressed in woman's clothes. He felt that she didn't love what was special about him, thus isolating him. He didn't feel any inner contradiction between his liking for women's clothes, jewellery, and make up, and love of his wife. He gradually learnt to love what his wife didn't like about his personality. It was then important for the wife to gain insight into her own otherness and particularity, intensifying a sense of what was distinctive in her own personality. Now each of them could devote themselves to essential inner aspects uncomprehended and unloved by the other. They thus developed sensitivity to what is radically other and strange in people as a whole, even if they didn't express that conceptually. This newly-gained sensitivity was a decisive step towards maturation for both of them, and their mutual love gained in depth and intensity. They lost the illusion of total agreement within love, and attained the insight that solitude and love are mutually dependent.

In his autobiographical piece *Solitary*, August Strindberg emphasises another value within solitude. Temporary withdrawal into solitude directs energy into fallow aspects of the personality, which would remain unlived if subjected to excessively powerful external influences. 'Spinning a cocoon with the silk of one's soul, pupating, and waiting for transformation' makes possible a reorientation based on one's own resources.[5] That is an aspect of solitude which C. G. Jung was the first to investigate in depth psychology. He called this 'progressive regression' – *reculer pour mieux sauter:* taking a few steps back so as to be able to jump better. Within the depths of our essential selves we find the elements for a creative fresh start.

Let's now turn to the question of how solitude can develop into love of another. A merely intellectual answer would be self-deception. Only by describing an experience can I hope that the spark leaps across to something similar experienced by the reader. So what is my experience of solitude? What happens to me if I don't reject solitude as something unsuitable but instead become one with it, thereby transmitting energy and making it capable of development? The answer to that question can be provided by *meditation,* viewed not as the contemplation or visualisation of images, but as in Buddhism (particularly Zen) as alert non-intervention, consciously allowing bodily processes to take place – above all the coming and going of the breath, paying relaxed, benevolent attention to what occurs within ourselves of its own accord, with the bodily posture furthering such attentiveness: sitting freely, with a straight but relaxed back, either on the heels, cross-legged, or in half-lotus position on a firm cushion. In such a primordial meditation we don't sink into ourselves but feel like a tiger about to leap, as Lama Sogyal Rimpoche once put it: completely relaxed and yet alert and highly sensitive to vital movements in the body and the outer world. In the breath that comes and goes we observe our powerful, unwavering will to life. We can do almost nothing but breathe. So let's unite with the breathing, which then becomes a profoundly fulfilling, deeply satisfying life-rhythm. Sounds from the outer world – all sounds without distinction, and not just those thought 'beautiful' – are also directly-sensed life: a woodpecker, a screaming child, a mother calling, an aeroplane, a metallic bang, and a car passing by. The chance succession and interaction of these very different sounds create a self-evident symphony.

Something even more remarkable occurs during this kind of meditation. The signs of life in one's own body and in the outer world become completely one, but not in the sense that we intermingle – as in a trance or dream – ourselves and the world as a cloudy mish-mash of experience. Relaxed attentiveness to everything happening – without the intervention of disturbing reflections – instead results in our self and the outer world merging as a comprehensive whole, a totality that we perceive both precisely and soberly, and also within the vital vibration of feelings, in every constellation that the present moment brings. At every moment we are aware of the whole through individual aspects which stimulate the senses.

The following passage by Jung, where he equates consciousness as comprehended in Indian philosophy and depth psychology's understanding of the unconscious, only applies to the trance experienced by Hindu yogis, and should not be taken as a generalisation covering all forms of Eastern meditation. He writes:

> They (the yogis) do not realise that a 'universal consciousness' is a contradiction in terms since exclusion, selection, and discrimination are the root and essence of everything that lays claim to the name 'consciousness'. 'Universal consciousness' is logically identical with unconsciousness . . . With increasing extension, the contents of consciousness lose in clarity of detail. In the end, consciousness becomes all-embracing but nebulous; an infinite number of things merge into an indefinite whole, a state in which subject and object are almost completely identical. That is all very beautiful but scarcely to be recommended anywhere north of the Tropic of Cancer.[6]

UNIVERSAL CONSCIOUSNESS

Many yogis and practitioners of Zen do not agree with Jung's evaluation of yoga meditation. For them meditation entails the experience of an enormous liberation with regard to the whole by way of as impartial and direct a perception as possible of individual aspects of what is happening in this moment. The nebulous remoteness from reality which for them constitutes normal consciousness is surpassed. The usual veils of repression and avoidance fall away in moments of open attentiveness. That is the source of the mediumistic clear-sightedness of people for whom meditation and active life have become one. They quickly grasp complex situations which others approach laboriously and unsuccessfully. Apart from the process of introspective work on repressions, traumas really can be provisionally annulled through conscious identification with what is happening in the moment as furthered by meditation. Speaking from the perspective of this second mediumistic way of becoming conscious of what has been repressed, we no longer seek to objectivise the unconscious and its contents but talk subjectively about an attitude of unconsciousness, which is the contrary of the intellectual clarity illuminating meditation. This intellectual clarity, where awareness of the universal and of the individual is identical, has become an everyday matter of course even for an increasing number of Westerners over the past twenty years. Such meditation involves universal consciousness of relationship, comprising the individual as a relational process within the whole and vice versa.

Jung's pupil Erich Neumann has already shown that an alertly receptive consciousness exists alongside the reflective consciousness, understanding the whole in terms of what is now happening. He called that the matriarchal consciousness.[7]

As meditation deepens, the world – the self and the other, what is inward and what is outward – becomes a single orchestra and a single symphony where the question of making distinctions between consonances and dissonances, harmony and disharmony, is never raised. The 'Great Yes' to everything that exists is also a 'Yes' to the 'No' – to all negative poles within the play of energies, to transience and death. The destructive rage separated from life melts into this great affirmation, increasingly transforming itself into a capacity to reach out and seize the possibilities life offers.

It thus becomes apparent during meditation that solitude and love of the other are identical. In letting go mine and yours, we discover that 'the substance of the universe cannot be torn' (Pierre Teilhard de Chardin); that being at home with oneself simultaneously means being in the

world, or, better still, being the world; that the body and
its sense organs, like the rest of the world, are connections, relationships, and pulsating energy; that there only
exists a *single* undivided love, namely love of all being; and
that, finally, love is nothing other than this alert, ardent
being within relationship, creating union. In moments of
'inner silence' a human being recognises the illusory nature of thoughts which cut him off from true life, from
love.[8]

Meditation doesn't cease after the twenty or thirty minutes
we 'sit' there. It is a comprehensive way of perceiving and
loving, which we once again bring back to mind clearly
through a 'special' meditation. It entails allowing to happen,
non-resistance, non-separation, and conscious relaxation, as
I demonstrated in mental massage which is also a kind of
meditation. It is the way of being which helps our world
onwards.

> Developments in the modern world have brought us to a
> point where the most external aspects (politics) and the most
> internal (meditation) speak the same language. Both circle
> around the basic principle that nothing but 'relaxation' can
> take us further. All mysteries involve the art of giving way
> and not resisting. . . . Today's big politics ultimately involves
> meditation on the bomb, and deep meditation searches out
> the bomb-building impulse within ourselves . . . The only
> question remains whether we choose the outer way or the
> inner – whether we gain insight from reflection or from balls
> of fire over the earth.[9]

So will relaxation come about through inner coming to terms
with ourselves or through an external catastrophe? The inner
way of relaxation involves love of all being, and the outer way
destruction of everything.

What is needed is the basic attitude of *composure* as comprehended by the Buddha and Heidegger. Composure entails
letting go of what my isolated will wants and accepting what
now wants to happen, being disposable, and allowing oneself
to be inspired by and to pursue the real. Meister Eckhart
speaks in that connection of not knowing, not having, and
not wanting. A psychology which follows the human subject

in everything and doesn't pass on the limitations of its own methods ends up in mysticism.

Ancient wisdom says that 'submission' in the sense of such composure and the most alert of activity do not exclude but rather condition one another. It's the highpoint of what Krishna has to teach Arjuna in the Bhagavad Gita, the central element in the *Mahabarata*, the Indian epic and 'gospel' of the Hindus. This message also touched Westerners directly in Jean-Claude Carrière's adaptation of the *Mahabarata* as staged by Peter Brook. In the dockside hall where the epic was performed in Zürich there prevailed a mood of exhilaration compounded of relaxed vitality, stimulating composure, and a heartfelt link between actors and audience such as I had never previously experienced. The performance was a shared meditation.

'Forget desire' – in other words, that isolated wanting which is not attuned to the overall situation – 'and seek detachment' is Krishna's demand of Arjuna. He means that Arjuna should forget egoistic motives and enter upon the unavoidable struggle with his relatives: submission to necessary activity. The decisive attitude there is composure. Krishna asks Arjuna: 'Can you fight without anger and pride?'[10] Can you struggle with composure?

IN UNION WITH THE WORLD

The true solitary renounces clinging onto people, habits of mind and feeling, ideologies and religions, or seeking a foothold wherever it may be. By attaining this renunciation, he liberates himself from the illusion of a world that appears to be separate and able to make up for something which he himself lacks. He is so inwardly and intimately linked with the world that it can no longer offer him any foothold or support since he is identical with union with the world, with the world as relationship, with the 'universally flowing subject'. Mark you, he doesn't inflate his subjectivity as far as the world extends. His subjectivity instead melts in the insight that identity, as Buber says, is in between, in relationship.

It is splendid to be solitary if the one in whom I am alone (all-one) is the world.

SIXTEEN

The Energetics of Love

'Liberation from ego-consciousness
is the greatest happiness'
Gautama Buddha

The way and objective I have followed in this book involved a process of unlocking the energy of love through devoting loving attention to the wound of our being unloved. A psychotherapy that doesn't become a psycho-energetics of love cannot help since healing only occurs by way of relationship as already clearly demonstrated in magnetism and the eighteenth century beginnings of psychotherapy (Chapter 4). Vitalisation of love leads to liberation from a long-suffered isolation. On the one hand, the feeling of isolation derives from bitter experiences – mainly in childhood and adolescence – of being left alone at decisive moments and over prolonged periods, of being misunderstood, ignored, neglected, and unloved. On the other hand, that feeling is common to all human beings rather than being limited to those whose lives were blocked and misdirected as a result of early traumatic experiences. It reflects the fundamental state of essential solitude. The human being one day finds himself or herself thrown into the world as a 'lifelong premature birth', feeling both familiar and strange, reflected both in the other and in a profound otherness. Either he rebels against this contradiction, becoming a dull optimist who denies the secret agony of being separated, or a boring pessimist who refuses security and closeness. Or else he affirms contradiction: love and remoteness from love, similarity and otherness, the warmth of being embraced and the coldness of empty space. Loving himself as a totality, he discovers a new love. He's left behind the old love with its holding and being held, clinging and constraint, and weakness and desperation. He now experiences a love that includes remoteness and being unloved, a love both sober and ardent that incorporates solitude, a love that isn't aiming at something specific and is therefore available and open, and a love that heals the wounds of love by loving even them.

LIBERATING FROM EGO-CONSCIOUSNESS

In this final chapter I will add to ideas that have already been presented, showing how this new, realistic love, which is no longer based on projections, fantasies, and denials, leads to liberation from a consciousness that brings about our isolation, from what Buddhism calls ego-consciousness. Liberation from such ego-consciousness is viewed as the greatest happiness. Yet from the standpoint of a psychology considering the human being from an objective distance, the expression *'liberation from ego-consciousness'* is sheer nonsense. How can an I liberated from awareness of itself register liberation from ego-consciousness? That lack of understanding is also apparent in Jung's declaration: 'An ego-less intellectual state can only be unconscious for us since there simply would not be any witness'. Remember Jung's similar views on meditation. But in the language of psycho-energetics, giving direct expression to the flow of events, the phrase 'liberation from ego-consciousness' is profound wisdom. It indicates the transition from a world of separable concepts, things, and bodies to a world of pure relationship where the only awareness is *consciousness of relationship* in which the ego-consciousness is dissolved. The 'witness' to this consciousness of relationship is not even 'I' but essentially one and the same perception shared by me and others.

Such language is only new in psychology. Mysticism has expressed itself in that way since time immemorial. Remarkably, the language of mysticism in a wide range of cultures is similar or even the same, sometimes in the most subtle of formulations. It seems as if ideological, religious, and political dependence is largely left behind in this language of mysticism. Doesn't psychotherapy also want to liberate people from alienating dependence? Wouldn't it also like to open up access to the human essence? Why therefore should it hold back from a therapeutically healing language? We must become aware that such a healing impact has also received expression in existing psychotherapy, especially when it touched upon profoundly essential experiences. Jung himself went this way in describing archetypal images. The language of mysticism is even more independent of culture and epoch since it reproduces fundamental human states rather than describing images. The myths of different peoples merely resemble each other whereas mystical trains of thought are almost everywhere.

I am not, however, maintaining that the objectivising language of psychotherapy is superfluous and meaningless. It is justified in terms of the need for an overall view and classification of psychological manifestations. But I don't conceal the fact that this need declines the more intensively and consciously we are immersed in life's flow of events. The differentiations available to a *language of events* are in no way inferior to those of a *language of order*. Quite the contrary in fact. Its adaptable flow subtly takes in all the unevennesses and formations in the area over which it moves. The practical necessity is to make a distinction between a language of order which reifies, distances, and is static in its descriptions of moving processes, and an experiential, immediate, and dynamic language of events. The former is reflection which distances itself from action, whereas the latter is action that elucidates and describes itself.

Too much thinking creates a distance from the reality thought about. Who doesn't know that unhappy species of student which wants to do some research particularly well, goes into ever greater detail, cuts itself off from the inner flow holding together the object at issue, and is finally left, despairing and paralysed, with the innumerable fragments produced by its eagerness. The appropriate closeness to the object is lacking. The same also applies to political problems. Anyone who thinks too much loses sight of the problem. Ji Wenzi, an excellent Chinese minister in the sixth century BC, always considered something three times before taking action. Confucius observed: 'Twice is absolutely sufficient'[1], since for Confucius considering three times entailed losing something of the sense of what is immediately involved. We are anxious about closeness, even in thinking.

The unloved think in the wrong moment. A woman told me that she often had the following thoughts during sexual encounters. 'Am I putting on a performance?', or 'Is my partner putting on an act?' While she thinks that, she loses all pleasure in sexuality. To the first question we can say: 'Yes, since you ask – it's always a performance. The question is itself part of that. There wasn't a performance before the question was put. The question serves your anxiety about intimacy'. The second question about whether her partner was putting on an act could perhaps be answered as follows: 'You're putting on a performance by asking this question. If you remained unquestioningly within the flow of your tender feelings, it wouldn't be important to you how far you get with your partner today. You would be identical with your relationship as it is at present'. Reflection at the wrong moment is loveless – towards both oneself and the other. Anyone who in moments of closeness thinks about himself or the other splits his consciousness away from the relationship. The natural consciousness of relationship becomes an artificial ego-consciousness. That is a characteristic of all *unloved games* (chapters 2 and 3).

This woman would, however, lack love for herself if she were now to torment and criticise herself for having raised this question. Defensive self-criticism takes you even further away from self-love. What is necessary now is also to affirm the distance-creating impulse so as to again become one and whole: 'That's all right. I raised the question'. This affirmation leads to momentary relaxation. The question is renounced, the ego relinquished. Desire for closeness arises again. The ego-consciousness expands into awareness of relationship.

The unloved lose consciousness of relationship more easily than others. The oldest of all psychological wounds, not being loved, can break open time and again (chapter 1). In the open wound of depression the emotional lack of relationship becomes a lasting state of affairs (chapter 7). If we isolate ourselves from other people while inwardly remembering early hurts, we experience the external world as unbearable pressure countering our impulse towards life (chapter 9). Instead of seeking contact on the erotic trail, we pursue the profoundly established traumatic trail of self-abandonment and lack of self-love (chapter 11). Our solitude is unfruitful because it cuts itself off from love (chapter 15).

EGO-STRENGTH

How does ego-consciousness express itself? In rigid *identifications*, which are usually called ego-strength. If, however, they come into conflict with reality, they turn out to be weaknesses. Fear of letting go of something familiar takes us ever further away from what wants to happen in our lives. It violently blocks the flow of life, believing that it can hold back the spring tide of vitality by means of this psychological dam. It allows identifications to take root. Salvation is linked with a single human being, a single religion or ideology, or with fixed ideas about ourselves (chapter 8) or our parents (chapter 6). Excessive importance is attributed to the ego. The emphasis with which excessively identified human beings say 'I' is disproportionate: 'I am afraid', 'I feel guilty', 'I absolutely want to achieve this or that', or 'I am lonely and abandoned'. When they speak that little word 'I', something tightens up inside. Anxiety about some threat or insecurity makes them tense and demanding. The other is faded out, and love falls silent.

What little support identifications provide! I identify with my thoughts, with my intelligence, an elevating feeling. Then I get violent stomach pains and can't think clearly any longer. I now couldn't care less about my intelligence. If I should have brain damage, what use would my intelligence be then? Or I identify with a good bodily presence and physical control. Great pain also dissolves that identification. Or I identify myself with a relationship with a certain person. That breaks down. Where am I then? Or I identify myself with my life. Then I become ill and die. Where is the ego that so clung to life? Anyone who doesn't free himself of ego-consciousness, expressing itself in rigid identifications, lives full of fear of losing whatever this 'ego' is. He won't be happy but rather fanatical in upholding walls and principles of belief. He wants to protect what he identifies with. Against what? Against *consciousness of relationship*.

Whatever we most violently resist often has in store the

greatest of happiness. As long as we identify with something, it doesn't give us any pleasure. There's too much anxiety in our clinging to it. But as soon as we yield inwardly, our pleasure is also liberated. We can most happily enjoy something where we don't feel any sense of dependence. Unplanned sex is most refreshing of all. A meeting I no longer expected is especially enjoyable. Fortunate coincidences enrich us from time to time with unforeseen happiness. A meditation during which the ego's identification with specific things is replaced by the feeling of *flow and balance* allows us an unequivocal experience of the happiness of freedom from ego-consciousness. The only real 'ego-strength' is to be found in this flow and balance. 'Support' doesn't lie in hanging onto something but in movement attuned to the overall situation. We then feel attracted towards that without any further effort on our part.

We are subject to innumerable *material constraints*. If we don't watch out, these become identifications. We then believe that we can't live without them any longer. It is, however, necessary to keep some areas free of such material constraints within the social landscape of an increasingly organised world, keeping them open and disposable as holy realms of creative emptiness where relationships and interconnections which we otherwise miss suddenly blaze up. We need times and spaces when we are simply there and available – in the same way as there must be zones within a landscape which are not built on. Real material constraints then also lose the character of painful identifications. We awaken from the *social hypnosis* which made us confuse our network of obligations with life itself.[2]

THE ESSENCE OF SELF-LOVE

Doesn't liberation from ego-consciousness also entail loss of self-love? That question provides me with an opportunity of pentrating more deeply into the essence of self-love. I distinguish between a real and an apparent self-love, between an open self-love and a narcissistic self-observation and self-reflection. The difference becomes immediately apparent in a striking autobiographical incident from Martin Buber's childhood:

During the summer holidays on my grandparent's estate, I used to creep into the stable – as often as I could without being observed – and fondle the neck of my darling, a fat dapple-grey horse. That was a deeply moving affair for me . . . not just a passing pleasure . . . What I experienced in this animal was the other, the enormous otherness of the other – without however remaining alien as with the ox or ram – which allowed me to approach and touch it . . . establishing an elementally close relationship with me . . . Once however . . . when I was stroking the animal . . . I realised what pleasure it gave me, and I suddenly felt my hand. The game carried on as usual, but something had changed. It was no longer That. And next day when I stroked my friend's neck after feeding him well, he did not raise his head.[3]

Real self-love cannot be distinguished from love of another. No distance exists between the one and the other. In touching the other I am moved. I'm close to myself when close to you. In a loving movement I am moved by love, am nothing but love – to myself as well – without thinking about that. There is no ego-consciousness that notices self-love, distinguishing itself from consciousness of another which establishes love of the other. Consciousness of relationship is love fully consummated and fully aware of what vibrated between the two, transforming you and me. This comes from the heart not the head – what Blaise Pascal called 'raison du coeur'. As a child completely involved in contact with the dapple-grey, Martin Buber first felt that self-forgetful love, identical with itself, which liberates from the ego-consciousness and is the greatest happiness. But one day that degenerated into vain self-satisfaction, an impoverished substitute with which those who have been deprived console themselves for lack of real self-love. Like all the unloved, he inclined towards self-observation at the wrong moment so as to assure himself that he really was loving – that his hand could stroke and he felt pleasure. His ego-consciousnesss was thus reinstated, and love died simultaneously. The horse felt that with its sure instinct, and no longer lifted its head. The child was once again caught up in its ego and had lost contact with the horse. With regard to that process there is no difference between the young Martin Buber's relationship to the dapple-grey and an adult's relationship to another person. Love and self-satisfaction exclude one another.

The therapist who participates in the suffering of an unloved child completely lets go of reflective distance at the moment of healing, sensing the feeling he wants to liberate in his client (Chapter 12).

In mental massage too, the cat, our body, only purrs if attention is devoted without any distancing self-reflection. The body becomes a closely related other which comes to life in this mental contact (Chapter 13).

What is decisive in the energetics of love is expansion of ego-consciousness to become a consciousness of relationship. That happens by renouncing reflective distance in whatever we are doing. Of course that doesn't mean that we should act rashly. Instead thought moves in conjunction with action, just as a rider is closely connected with his horse's movements. Action moves to the centre of attention. Moshe Feldenkrais, the movement therapist, writes:

Unless a stage is reached at which self-regard ceases to be the main motivating force, any improvement achieved will never be sufficient . . . In fact, as a man grows and improves, his entire existence centres increasingly on what he does and how, while who does it becomes of ever decreasing importance.[4]

When doing something I am linked with the whole world. Within myself the world comes to itself, and in the world I come alive. Action in which I lose myself is devotion. That is only possible so long as I am not forced away in my thoughts from what is here and now, backward into the past or forward into the future. But then, in the experience of being present within myself without taking thought, love awakens. Space opens up. The world expands. Someone liberated into love feels unrestricted. Breathing – the inner wind as Tibetans call it – becomes one with the world's other rhythms, uniting with their rise and fall.

Has the wound of being unloved now been healed once and for all? How could that be since the traumatic traces of earlier lovelessness are never completely wiped out, and the feeling of strangeness is a fundamental aspect of the human condition! Time and again the wound of being unloved will reappear at the crucial moments of life. But we know the direction we're taking. Once again we'll let go of a dependence so as to make love possible. The wound of being unloved is the womb out of which we are born many times over.

Notes

CHAPTER 1. THE OLDEST WOUND

1. Buddha, Gautama, *The Four Noble Truths*
2. Sloterdijk, P. *Der Zauberbaum*, p. 253
3. On the problem of shame see Hultberg, P. *'Scham – Eine Überschattete* Emotion', in: *Zeitschrift für Analytische Psychologie*, July 1987, pp. 84–104
4. Mahler, M.S. *On Human Symbiosis and the Vicissitudes of Individuation*
5. ibid.

CHAPTER 2. 'THE WRONG PERSON AGAIN!' AND OTHER UNLOVED GAMES

1. Zundel, E. & R. *Leitfiguren der Psychotherapie*, p. 149

CHAPTER 3. 'EVERYBODY LOVES ME' AND OTHER UNLOVED GAMES

1. Watzlawick, P. *Ultra Solutions*
2. Wieck, W. *Männer lassen lieben*
3. cf. Schellenbaum, P. 'Heilende Impulse aus der winzigen, weichen Bewegung', in: *Abschied von der Selbstzerstörung*, pp. 192–205

CHAPTER 4. PSYCHO-ENERGETICS

1. cf. Schellenbaum, P. *Abschied von der Selbstzerstörung*, p. 37 f.
2. quoted in: Zundel, E & R. *Leitfiguren der Psychotherapie*, p. 152 f.
3. Eckhart, Meister *Sermons and Treatises*
4. Sloterdijk, P. *Der Zauberbaum*, p. 185
5. ibid, p. 188
6. See bibliography: Mesmer, F.A.; Kaly; Josipovici, J.; Zweig, S.; Schott, H.; Sloterdijk, P., (*Der Zauberbaum*)

7.   cf. Sloterdijk, P. *Der Zauberbaum*, p. 250 f.
8.   Mesmer, F.A. *Abhandlung über die Entdeckung des thierischen Magnetismus*, p. 12, 20, 46 f.
9.   Kaly, *Initiation au Magnétisme*, pp. 28–33
10.   Jospovici, J., Mesmer, F.A. *magnétiseur, médicin et francmaçon*, pp. 188–194
11.   cf. Schott, H. *Über den thierischen Magnetismus und sein Legitimationsproblem*, p. 104 with note 7
12.   Störig, H.J. *Kleine Weltgeschichte der Philosophie*, p. 456
13.   Quoted from Schott, H. op. cit., p. 110 f
14.   Zweig, S. *Heilung durch den Geist*, p. 220
15.   Nietzsche, F. *Der Wille zur Macht*

CHAPTER 5. LOVE OF OUTCASTS

1.   Schwarzenau, P. *Das göttliche Kind*, pp. 17–25
2.   Watts, A. *Psychotherapy East and West*, p. 85

CHAPTER 6. RENUNCIATION OF BELATED PARENTAL LOVE

1.   Sloterdijk, P. *Der Zauberbaum*, p. 189
2.   Nietzsche, F. *Thus Spake Zarathustra*
3.   Nietzsche, F. *Über Wahrheit und Lüge im außermoralischen Sinn*
4.   Nietzsche, F. *Thus Spake Zarathustra*
5.   Jung, C.G. *Symbols of transformation*, p. 414
6.   ibid, p. 415
7.   ibid, p. 418

CHAPTER 7. THE OPEN WOUND OF DEPRESSION

1.   Freud, S. *Mourning and Melancholia*
2.   ibid
3.   ibid
4.   ibid
5.   ibid
6.   Buddha, Gautama *The Four Noble Truths*

CHAPTER 8. IDENTITY IN LONGING

1.   Nietzsche, F. *Abschied von der Metaphysik*
2.   Fetscher, R. *Selbst und Identität*, in: *Psyche*, May 1983, p. 397
3.   ibid, p. 398
4.   ibid, p. 399
5.   Weber, S.M. *Rückkehr zu Freud*, p. 14

6. ibid, p. 14
7. cf. Schellenbaum, P. *Die Homosexualität des Mannes*, and *Stichwort: Gottesbild*
8. cf. Schellenbaum, P. *How to Say No to the One You Love*, and *Abschied von der Selbstzerstörung*

CHAPTER 9. PRESSURE AND IMPULSE

1. Sloterdijk, P. *Critique of Cynical Reason*
2. ibid
3. ibid
4. Sloterdijk, P. *Der Zauberbaum*
5. Freud, S. *Civilisation and Its Discontents*
6. Cheng, A. (ed.) *Entretiens de Confucius*, trans. P. Schellenbaum, p. 57
7. Jürg Willi views *collusion* as the most unconscious game played by partners. They do so in order to defend themselves against and surmount shared fears and guilt feelings. They cannot renounce collusion because it makes them feel linked by destiny. (Jürg Willi, *Couples in Collision*)
8. Sloterdijk, P. *Der Zauberbaum*, p. 224
9. cf. Lowen, A. *Bioenergetics*
10. Nietzsche, F. *Thus Spake Zarathustra*, Part III
11. Lowen, A. op. cit.
12. Nietzsche, F. *The Gay Science*

CHAPTER 10. THE WORD BECOMES FLESH.

1. Jung, C.G. *The Spiritual Problem of Modern Man*, Collected Works, vol. 10 pp. 94–5
2. Cheng, A. (ed.) *Entretiens de Confucius*, trans. P. Schellenbaum
3. Sloterdijk, P. *Der Denker auf der Bühne*, p. 137 & 140
4. Sloterdijk, P. *Critique of Cynical Reason*, vol. 2

CHAPTER 11. TRAUMATIC AND EROTIC PATTERNS

1. On the traumatic pattern cf. Frischknecht, M. *Die Verzauberung der Therapie*, a conversation with P. Sloterdijk, in: *Spuren* No. 2, Jan 1986, p. 5
2. Nietzsche, F. *Thus Spake Zarathustra*
3. cf. the myth of crossing the sea by night
4. Schellenbaum, P. *Homosexualität des Mannes*, p. 203 f.

Notes

CHAPTER 12. PARTICIPATION IN THE SUFFERING OF
THE UNLOVED CHILD

1. Meierhofer, M. & Keller, W. *Frustration im frühen Kindes-alter*, p. 223
2. Spitz, R. *Die Entstehung der ersten Objektbeziehungen*
3. Schellenbaum, P. *Abschied von der Selbstzerstörung*, pp. 168–171
4. cf. Kopp, S.B. *If You Meet the Buddha On the Road*

CHAPTER 14. LOVE IS ABNORMAL

1. Schellenbaum, P. *How To Say No To The One You Love*
2. Cheng, A. *Entretiens de Confucius*, trans. P. Schellenbaum, p. 58
3. Watts, A. *Psychotherapy East and West*, p. 47

CHAPTER 15. ESSENTIAL SOLITUDE

1. Nietzsche, F. *Thus Spake Zarathustra*
2. Sloterdijk, P. *Der Denker auf der Bühne*, p. 72
3. Buber, M. *Begegnung*, p.10 f.
4. cf. Schellenbaum, P. *Abschied von der Selbstzerstörung*, pp. 163–8
5. Strindberg, A. *Einsam – Autobiographische Schrift*
6. Jung, C.G. *Conscious, Unconscious, and Individuation*, C.W. 9/1, pp. 287–8
7. cf. Neumann, E. *The Origins and History of Consciousness*
8. Pirandello, L. *L'umorismo*
9. Sloterdijk, P. *Critique of Cynical Reason*, Vol. 1
10. Carrière, J.-C. *The Mahabarata*. On the dialogue between Krishna and Arjuna cf. Schellenbaum, P. *Stichwort: Gottesbild*, pp. 181–8

CHAPTER 16. THE ENERGETICS OF LOVE

1. Cheng, A. *Entretiens de Confucius*, trans. P. Schellenbaum, p. 52
2. cf. Watts, A. *Psychotherapy East and West*, p. 80
3. Buber, M. *Begegnung*, p. 25 f.
4. Feldenkrais, M. *Awareness through Movement*, p. 19

Bibliography

Andreas-Salomé, L. *Lebensrükblick*, Frankfurt, 1974.
Bhagavad Gita, Harmondsworth, 1970.
Boyesen, G. *Über den Körper die Seele heilen*, Munich, 1987.
Buddha, G. *The Dhammapada*, Harmondsworth, 1983.
Buber, M. *Hinweise*, Zürich, 1973.
—, *The Way of Man*, London, 1963.
—, *The Life of Dialogue*, Chicago, 1976.
—, *Begegnung – Autobiographische Fragmente*, Heidelberg, 1986.
Carrière, J.-C. *The Mahabarata*, London, 1988.
de Chardin, P. Teilhard *Oeuvres 1–10*, Paris, 1955–1965.
Cheng, A. *Entretiens de Confucius*, Paris, 1981.
Coliodi, C. *Pinocchio*, London, 1986.
Eckhart, Meister *Sermons and Treatises*, Shaftesbury, 1987.
Eliade, M. *The Myth of the Eternal Return*, London, 1989.
Erikson, E.H. *Identity and the Life Cycle*, New York, 1980.
Evers, T. *Mythos und Emanzipation*, Hamburg, 1987.
Feldenkrais, M. *Awareness through Movement*, Harmondsworth, 1987.
Fetscher, R. 'Das Selbst und das Ich', in: *Psyche 5*, vol. 35, July 1981, Stuttgart.
—, 'Selbst und Identität', in: *Psyche 7*, vol. 37, May 1983, Stuttgart.
Flach, F.F. *Depression als Lebenschance*, Hamburg, 1985.
Freud, A. *The Ego and the Mechanisms of Defence*, New York, 1966.
Freud, S. *Collected Works*, London, 1955–1966.
—, *Psycho-analysis and faith. The letters of Sigmund Freud and Oskar Pfister*, New York, 1963.
Frey-Rohn, L. *Jenseits der Werte Seiner Zeit; Friedrich Nietzsche im Spiegel seiner Werke*, Zürich, 1984.
Frischknecht, M. 'Die Verzauberung der Therapie, Gespräch mit P. Sloterdijk' in: *Spuren* No. 2, Zürich, 1986.
Frisch, M. *Andorra*, London, 1985.
Graves, R. *Greek Mythology*, vols. 1 & 2, Harmondsworth, 1955.
Green, E. & A. *Biofeedback*, New York,
Grof, S. *Birth, Death, and Transcendence*, New York,
Gruen, A. *Der Verrat am Selbst*, Munich, 1986.
—, *Der Wahnsinn der Normalität*, Munich, 1987.
Huang, Al *Embrace Tiger, Return to Mountain: Essence of Tai Chi*, Berkeley, 1988.
Josipovici, J. *Franz-Anton Mesmer, magnétiseur, médicin, et francmaçon*, Monaco, 1982.

Bibliography

Jung, C.G. *Collected Works*, London, 1953–1971.
Kafka, F. *America*, Harmondsworth, 1970.
Kaltenmarte, O. (Ed.), *La littérature chinoise*, Paris, 1977.
Kaly, *Initiation au magnetisme*, Paris, 1982.
Kalpan, P. *The Three Pillars of Zen*, London, 1988.
Kérenyi, K. *Gods of the Greeks*, London, 1974.
Klein, M. *Psychoanalysis of Children*, London, 1959.
Kohut, H. *The Analysis of the Self*, New York, 1971.
—, *The Restoration of the Self*, New York, 1977.
Kopp, S.B. *If You Meet the Buddha on the Road, Kill Him*, London, 1974.
Krishna, G. *Kundalini*, London,
Lacan, J. *Works*, London, 1988.
Lowen, A. *Love and Orgasm*, London, 1976.
—, *Narcissism*, London, 1985.
—, *Bioenergetics*, Harmondsworth, 1979.
Maertens, J.-T. *Ritanalyses 1*, Paris, 1987.
Mahler, M.S. *On Human Symbiosis and the Vicissitudes of Individuation*, New York, 1968.
Meirhofer, M. & Keller, W. *Frustration im frühen Kindesalter*, Beren, 1974.
Mesmer, F.A. *Abhandlung über die Entdeckung des thierischen Magnetismus*, Tübingen, 1984.
Mitscherlich, A. & M. *The Inability to Mourn*, New York, 1985.
Moravia, A. *Agostino*,
Neumann, E. *The Child*, New York, 1988.
—, *The Origins and History of Consciousness*, London, 1982.
—, *The Great Mother*, London, 1982.
Nietzsche, F. *Die Philosophie im tragischen Zeitalter der Griechen*, Munich, 1921.
—, *The Gay Science*, New York, 1974.
—, *Beyond Good and Evil*, New York, 1968.
—, *Der Wille zur Macht*, Munich, 1926.
—, *Thus Spake Zarathustra*, Harmondsworth, 1969.
—, *The Anti-Christ*, Harmondsworth, 1969.
—, *The Birth of Tragedy*, New York, 1968.
Norwood, R. *Women Who Love Too Much*, London, 1986.
Perls, F.S. *Gestalt Therapy*, London, 1984.
Pirandello, L. *L'umorismo*,
Proust, M. *Remembrance of Things Past*, Harmondsworth, 1983.
Frh.v. Reichenbach, K.L. *Der sensitive Mensch und sein Verhalten zum Ode*, vols. 1 & 2, Stuttgart, 1854.
Rieger, D. (Ed.), *Französische Chansons*, Stuttgart, 1987.
de Ronsard, P. *Amours*, Lausanne, 1964.
Sabetti, S. *Lebensenergie*, Munich, 1985.
Schellenbaum, P. *Le Christ dans l'Energétique teilhardienne*, Paris, 1971.
—, 'Die Christologie des Teilhard de Chardin', in: *Theol. Berichte II*, Zürich, 1973.
—, *Homosexualität des Mannes*, Munich, 1980.
—, *Stichwort: Gottesbild*, Stuttgart, 1981.
—, *How to Say No to the One You Love*, Illinois,
—, *Abschied von der Selbstzerstörung*, Stuttgart, 1987.

The Wound of the Unloved

Schott, H. (Ed.), *Franz Anton Mesmer und die Geschichte des Mesmerismus*, Stuttgart, 1985.

Schwarzenau, P. *Das göttliche Kind*, Stuttgart, 1984.

Sloterdijk, P. *Critique of Cynical Reason*, London, 1984.

—, *Der Zauberbaum*, Frankfurt, 1986.

—, *Der Denker auf der Bühne – Nietzsches Materialismus*, Frankfurt, 1986.

Spielrein, S. *Die Destruktion als Ursache des Werdens*, Tübingen, 1986.

Spitz, R. *Die Entstehung der ersten Objektbeziehungen*, Stuttgart, 1966.

Störig, H.J. *Kleine Weltgeschichte der Philosophie*, Frankfurt, 1987.

Strindberg, A. *Einsam – Autobiographische Schrift*, Munich, 1961.

Tolstoy, L.N. *Anna Karenina*, Harmondsworth, 1984.

Tse, Lao *Tao Te Ching*, Harmondsworth, 1986.

Watts, A. *The Book*, New York, 1969.

—, *Om. Creative Meditations*, Berkeley, 1980.

—, *Psychotherapy East and West*, New York, 1969.

—, *The Way of Zen*, Harmondsworth, 1965.

Watzlawick, P. *Change*, New York, 1980.

—, *Ultra Solutions: How To Fail Most Successfully*, New York, 1988.

Weber, S.M. *Rück-kehr zu Freud, Jacques Lacans Ent-stellung der Psychoanalyse*, Frankfurt, 1978.

Werfel, F. *Der Abituriententag*, Vienna, 1958.

Wieck, W. *Männer lassen lieben*, Stuttgart, 1987.

Wilde, O. *De Profundis*, Harmondsworth, 1973.

Willi, J. *Couples in Collision*, London, 1979.

Winicott, D.W. *Maturational Processes and the Facilitating Environment*, London, 1965.

Zimmer, H. *Myths and Symbols in Indian Art and Civilisation*, Princeton, 1971.

Zundel, E. & R. *Leitfiguren der Psychotherapie*, Munich, 1987.

Zweig, S. *Die Heilung durch den Geist*, Frankfurt, 1986.